Give Your Kids a Sporting Chance

Give Your Kids a Sporting Chance

A Parents' Guide

Kevin S. Spink PhD

Summerhill Press
Toronto

Published by Summerhill Press Ltd.
Toronto, Ontario

Printed and bound in Canada

Canadian Cataloguing in Publication Data

Spink, Kevin S., 1952-
    Give your kids a sporting chance

ISBN 0-920197-43-4

1. Sports for children. 2. Sports for children - Psychological aspects. I. Title.

GV709.2.S68 1988   796'.01'922   C88-093483-2

Preface

For a number of years now I have been working with elite athletes from a variety of sports. While I have learned a number of facts about these individuals during this time, the one that is most vivid in my mind concerns parental involvement. With very few exceptions, these athletes, be they professional or Olympic competitors, have all enjoyed the benefit of a home environment that was supportive and encouraging. In fact, from what the athletes have told me, to say that proper parental involvement was a benefit may not be strong enough. It was more like a prerequisite. Getting to the top would not have been possible without the strong support from their parents.

The powerful, positive effect that parents can have on athletes is not limited to elite athletes. It permeates all levels of sport. My work with children participating in age-group sports has revealed a similar phenomenon. Those kids who are getting the most out of their sporting experience are also the ones who have the strongest parental support.

It is refreshing to know that a child's sporting experience may be positively influenced by parents. I say refreshing because one would certainly not get that impression by reading media reports. Quite the opposite, in fact. Open the papers and you can read about the father who bit off an umpire's ear to protest a poor call being made against his son's team, or about the mother who falsified her son's birth certificate so he could star in a younger age group, or about the father who was yelling for a penalty call when his son was injured, while a mother from the opposing team, retorted "If they [the children] are going to give it, they better learn how to take it." Such stories certainly do not cast parents in the best light.

For the last several years, given both the positive effect parents can have and the negative ways they sometimes act, I have been trying to identify the characteristics of good sporting parents. During this period I have interviewed literally hundreds of children and their parents about what constitutes a good sporting experience.

I have drawn two major conclusions from this work. First, the vast majority of parents are extremely well-intentioned when it comes to helping their children enjoy a positive sporting experience. Even in the media reports just mentioned, it is likely that the parents involved thought that they were doing the right thing, that is, protecting their child's interests. This brings me to my second conclusion and the primary reason why I wrote this book. While most parents think that they are acting in their child's best interest, most do not fully understand and/or tend to underestimate the impact of their words and actions on their child's development, both on and off the sporting field.

This book attempts to outline what "good" sporting parents seem to be doing that the rest are not, and to elaborate on why their actions and words work, using relevant psychological theory and concrete suggestions from the kids themselves.

I focus not just on the more obvious forms of sport-related behavior, such as acting appropriately at your child's games or practices, although these are very important, but also on some of the more subtle forms of off-field behavior. I'm going to be looking at such questions as how to help your child keep sport in perspective, the degree to which you can, or should, "push" your child to improve, and the best ways to help them cope with defeat.

Whether you are a parent with a child who is climbing to the top rung of the sport ladder—or has aspirations to do this—or you are the parent of a child who is simply playing at a recreational level, this book has something to offer to you. And the information provided will not only enhance your child's sport experiences but will also provide your child with "a sporting chance" at life itself. For, like it or not, sport is in many ways a mirror of life itself and many of the lessons that we learn through sport—the value of cooperation and the benefits of hard work, for instance—transfer to endeavors off the field. In fact, this connection between sport and the other aspects of our lives is the subject of the first chapter.

Finally, I would like to close this preface on a personal note: To my parents, in case you're wondering, you did "give your kid a sporting chance."

TABLE OF CONTENTS

CHAPTER ONE
A Sporting Life

"A winning desire should be stressed at all levels, but it shouldn't be a life-and-death situation. Simply give your best and have fun doing it." *Gordie Howe, Former Ice-Hockey Star.*

What do you want for your children? If you're like most parents, you probably harbor some secret desires. While these may vary from one family to another, one aspiration tends to permeate the dreams of most parents—the desire to see their children get ahead in life.

We realize that for them to get ahead in life, we must provide children with the best opportunities in their formative years: the best education we can afford (and, in some cases, that we cannot afford), the best medical care available, the best equipment and facilities available—to name only a few items that most parents perceive as important.

But what about providing the best sporting experience? How do you rate in that regard? And why should sport even be included in an important list such as this?

Why Sport?

How important is a sporting experience in the life of a child? At the risk of putting the horse before the cart, a more basic question may be, how important is sport in our society? According to the findings contained in the *Miller Lite Report on American Attitudes Toward Sports - 1983*, sport plays a vitally important and satisfying role in the lives of many people. This full-scale national survey of sports attitudes and practices in the United States provides dramatic evidence that a majority of people are very strongly influenced by sport.—fewer than 4 percent of Americans do not participate either as fans or athletes more than once a month.

More specifically, it was revealed that about 70 percent of all people participate in an athletic activity at least once a week, while a similar percentage either watch, read, or talk about sport with their friends on a daily basis.

If you still need convincing as to the pervasiveness of sport in our lives, you might want to take the following simple quiz:

What was the major accomplishment of the following individuals?

1. Dennis Conner
2. Carl Lewis
3. Mary Lou Retton
4. Sir Frederick Banting or Charles Best
5. Louis Pasteur
6. Robert Jarvik

If you come into regular contact with the print or electronic media, you likely found it easier to identify the accomplishments of the first three people listed than the last three. Is that because the athletic accomplishments of Conner, Lewis, and Retton were greater than the non-athletic feats of Banting, Pasteur, and Jarvik? When you think how the accomplishments of those last three people have combined to protect the health and welfare of much of the world's population through the development of insulin, pasteurization, and the artificial heart, the answer is obviously *no*. So why do sports hold such a valued place in our society?

Well, there's is no one answer to this question, and this book won't attempt to give all the possible answers. However, when you realize that the Super Bowl annually draws one of the largest television audiences, sport heroes are regularly feted with tickertape parades, and national holidays are called to celebrate sporting triumphs (such as the 1983 "unofficial" public holiday in Australia to celebrate that country's success in the

America's Cup yachting race), there can be little argument that sport occupies an important place in our collective psyche.

What About the Kids?

As you might imagine, this romance with sports is not restricted to adults. Parents pass on their interest in sports to their children. The *Miller Lite* findings revealed that 75 percent of parents encourage their children to participate in sports, while only 6 percent encourage their children to spend less time playing them. Seventy-five percent of parents indicated that they sometimes or frequently engage in some kind of sporting activity with their children.

Children and adolescents are also very aware of the importance placed on sport in our society. A study on the values of high school students conducted a number of years ago by James Coleman found that students valued athletic prowess much more than academic achievement. In response to the question, "How would you like to be remembered?" Coleman discovered that 44 percent wanted to be remembered as an athletic star, 31 percent as a brilliant student and and 25 percent as the most popular student. In other words, most kids would rather be a sports star than a star intellectual! Although this study was initially done in the 1960s, it was replicated 15 years later with the same result (Eitzen, 1975).

When we question children today about their heroes, some of them are invariably people involved in sports. The *Miller Lite Report* found that 60 percent of adults agree that athletes are often the best role models a child can have.

So sports, whether we like it or not, are a pervasive force in our society. This pervasiveness begs a more important question: How important is the sporting experience in the life of a child?

The Value of Sport

Many North Americans believe that there is nothing more basic to child rearing than having their children participate in organized sports. But what evidence do we have to support such a belief?

In fact evidence suggests that sport can affect a child both positively and negatively. This may sound a little perplexing, but it is easily explained when we understand that the sporting environment is, in effect, neutral, neither inherently good nor bad for children. Rather, it is the adults who organize and supervise who create a "good" or "bad" environment for the children involved.

Here is an example that dramatically demonstrates this potential for positive and negative influences. Children who play for a coach who is continually "bending" the rules to secure a victory are likely to learn that cheating is acceptable if it enhances one's chances of winning. Coaches who play by the rules, on the other hand, convey that doing one's best under the circumstances is all that can be asked of anyone. Obviously, the children playing under these two coaches are presented with different views on morality. Note that it is not the sport, per se, that created these differences, but the way it was supervised.

Having acknowledged that some sports experiences can be bad for a child, it should be emphasized that a sporting program that is properly structured can provide some very positive spin-offs for the children involved, some of which are outlined below.

Children involved in sports are forced to learn the virtues of self-discipline. Olympic gold medal winner Alex Baumann revealed in a recent television interview that one of the most important lessons he learned from sport was the need for self-discipline. There is no reason why the self-discipline learned in the sports setting will not carry over into adulthood. This is likely one of the lessons that is alluded to when an individual such as the former Australian tennis star John Newcombe tells us that the lessons he learned in sport have helped him in his later-life business career.

Sports can also serve as an appropriate outlet for dissipating youthful "energy." You don't have to be around children very long to realize that they like to be active. Sports provide a much more acceptable and productive channel for this energy than the myriad of anti-social outlets available to children "with time on their hands." Statistics consistently reveal a lower incidence of juvenile delinquency in child athletes than in the general population. This finding was echoed in a recent interview with former hockey superstar Bobby Orr, who wondered what street corner he would have been on if he hadn't been involved in hockey.

Being active also appears to have some long-term benefits. Experts conclude that active children tend to have fewer behavioral problems as adults. They tend to be more sociable and cooperative and confident when they get older.

In physical terms, participation in sports results in a number of positive consequences. An active sports program, for instance, can contribute to good muscle tone, strong and healthy bones and joints, and a good level of physical fitness.

The need for a child to participate in sport for reasons of physical fitness is pressing because a large number of children do not receive any daily physical education. The President's Council on Physical Fitness and Sports and the National Center for Health Statistics recently revealed that only 36 percent of six to seventeen year olds in the U.S.A. participate in daily physical education programs in the schools. In elementary schools, half of the students attend such classes only once or twice a week, and the figures drop sharply after that. A similar pattern emerges in Canada, where physical education is also not compulsory in the schools.

Sport can also teach the basic, but important, psychomotor skills such as running, throwing, jumping, and hand-eye coordination. These are skills that, if learned early, can form the basis of an active lifestyle as an adult.

There is also evidence that athletes are often healthier psychologically than non athletes (Mehrabian & Bekken, 1986). From a psychological perspective, sport can significantly influence the development of a child's self-esteem.

Self-esteem

What is self-esteem and why is it important? Self-esteem is the value that people place on themselves and their behavior. It can be measured by finding out whether people feel good or bad about themselves.

Children with high self-esteem are generally satisfied with themselves and with their accomplishments. They willingly accept favorable feedback about themselves and reject negative feedback that might come their way. Children with low self-esteem, on the other hand, have negative feelings about themselves because they generally have a history of failure.

People are not born with a specific level of self-esteem. Self-esteem develops as we gain more and more experience of the world. Since children have limited experience, they tend to form opinions about themselves based on what the important people in their lives say to them or about them. Parents, obviously, figure very prominently in this. If parents consistently tell their children that they have "done well," "tried hard," "given it all they could," the children are likely to develop a high level of self-esteem. If, on the other hand, they hear from their parents that they "are no good," "could have done better," or "are losers," then, not surprisingly, these children develop lower levels of self-esteem. Parents influence the development of their children's self-esteem in other ways too. These will be discussed in a later chapter.

Why is self-esteem so important? Quite simply, what we think and feel about ourselves often influences how we function in the world. For instance, John, a young swimmer with high self-esteem, dismisses a loss as an experience to be learned from, whereas Mike, a swimmer with low self-esteem, views a loss as a confirmation of how bad he really is. His confidence in his ability to be a successful swimmer is thus further eroded.

Why might Mike think like this? People with low self-esteem will likely accept negative and reject positive feedback about themselves. This results in a "no win" situation. Mike is unlikely to increase his self-esteem because he'll resist any suggestion that he contributed to a success, but he'll willingly perceive failure as yet another indication that he really is "hopeless." Obviously, this is not a very good situation for children to find themselves in. The following chapters contain a number of suggestions that will help parents to alter this debilitating cycle.

The Sports Connection

The development of self-esteem is often closely linked to a child's sports involvement. There are a number of reasons for this.

It has been demonstrated that activities that society at large defines as meaningful play a more significant role in the development of self-esteem than non-meaningful activities do. Since sport is generally perceived to be important in our society, the successes and failures experienced in sport strongly influence the development of self-esteem.

Since children generally enter sports at the same time that they are beginning to form a stable conception of who they are and how they feel about themselves, the sporting experience can contribute significantly to the development of self-esteem.

There is evidence that sports enhance self-esteem. In one study, 300 children, some athletes and some non-athletes, were administered a self-esteem inventory (Purdon, 1978). The results revealed that the athletes had higher levels of self-esteem than the non-athletes at ages ten and thirteen years, but not at sixteen years, suggesting that the experiences children have in their early days of sport may contribute significantly to the enhancement of their self-esteem.

Another way in which sports build children's self-esteem is that children form opinions of themselves based on comparisons with others. This process of comparison starts around four or five years of age and peaks at about ten or eleven years of age—the age range in which most children enter sport.

Sporting activities provide many opportunities for children to compare themselves with others: Can I kick farther? Can I run faster? Can I throw straighter? Can I serve better? These are just a few of the questions children ask to determine where they stand relative to others. If the comparison is favorable in relation to these valued skills, then their self-esteem is likely to be enhanced. If the comparison is unfavorable, then their self-esteem is likely to suffer.

Sports *will* provide an appropriate environment for the development of self-esteem if children, during this critical stage, are helped to understand such comparisons in the most beneficial way. The role that parents can play in this regard is discussed in later chapters.

It is important to note that the self-esteem developed through sport is likely to spill over into other areas of the child's life, making the sports experience even more important.

Finally, in addition to these important "practical" benefits that result from involvement in sport, one should not forget that sport is generally a fun experience for children.

What's Wrong With Playing the Flute?

If sport is such a great institution, should we mandate it for all our children? Can we assume that individuals who grow up without participating in any sport will grow up in someway depressed or less fulfilled? I don't think so! I am sure we are all aware of perfectly functioning adults who would not know the difference between a double fault and foot fault.

Not every child is interested in sport. Based on a combination of factors, including the child's competencies, personality, friends and interests, it is quite possible that a child may be more interested in playing the flute, painting pictures, or rebuilding a car. If the child's interest is in other activities, parents should not be concerned. Sport is not for everyone; forcing children into a sport against their will often results in an unpleasant experience for everyone involved. If, on the other hand, the child's interest in sport has been dampened by negative experiences, then some self-analysis by the parents may be in order. The information contained in the remainder of this book should be of help in this regard.

A Very Big Team

While it is true that some children do not participate in sport, a very large number do. The findings of the *Miller Lite Report* reveal that approximately 60 percent of parents say their children participate in sport on a daily basis and of these, 83 percent of parents say at least some of these activities are competitive (i.e., involving meets, tournaments, etc.). Collectively, these children represent a very large team.

Such participation involves a considerable time commitment on the child's part. Any parent who has ever had a child in age-group swimming or little-league baseball will be very aware of this. But, whether we like it or not, a large number of children will, for better or for worse, be involved in organized sport at some point in their formative years. That's where parents come in!

Parent Power

Research reveals that parents play a critical role in a child's sporting experience, ranging from whether children get involved in sport at all, to their choice of sporting activity, to how the experience turns out. This last point forms the focus for this book, but a few comments about the selection of an appropriate sporting activity are in order.

Selecting a Sport

The most important factor to consider in the selection of a sport is your child's desires. While the final responsibility rests with the parents, the child's wishes, particularly their basic motives in selecting a sport, should be considered in the final decision. For instance, it would be wrong for a parent to place a child in an individual sport, such as tennis, when the child's primary motivation for participating in sport was to achieve a sense of belonging. This would be more readily accomplished in a team sport, such as hockey, where "we" feelings are generated as a matter of course.

Parents should not assume that they know what their children's motives for participation are. They need to ask their children what they want from sport, before an appropriate decision is made. More will be said about children's motives for participation in a later chapter.

Timing

Another decision to be made concerns the best age for children to enter competition. A recent survey of Canadian sports revealed that the average age of beginning competitors was nine years, although the age of entry into specific sports ranged from six to sixteen years. Statistics from the United States reveal that children enter sport at even earlier ages. In sports such as gymnastics and swimming, children start organized competition as young as three years.

With such a range of ages, what is the right age to enter competition? Quite simply, there is no single right age for all children to enter all sports. However, a consideration of the following factors should help in the decision.

First, parents should not force children into competition before the children themselves have indicated a willingness to participate. Children mature at different rates, and as a result, some feel a need to compete much earlier than others. Notwithstanding this, the earliest age that any child should be allowed to compete in organized sport, according to sport psychologist Michael Passer, is seven or eight years of age.

Second, the demands of the sport itself also need to be taken into account. Non-contact sports, such as baseball and tennis, obviously place different physical demands on a child than do contact sports, such as soccer and wrestling. These are different again from collision sports, such as ice hockey and football. Exercise specialists and medical experts recommend that entry into contact and collision sports should be delayed. Children younger than eight to ten years should be discouraged from participating in contact sports, and children younger than ten to twelve years should be discouraged from participation in collision sports. Children who are late developers physically should also be dissuaded from entering contact and collision sports until their bodies have matured physically. The problems associated with different rates of maturation will be discussed in a later chapter.

The guidelines stated above represent the *minimum* ages at which children should enter organized sports. There is no need to rush children into the competitive setting. Children need time to enjoy the experience of free play, either alone or in the company of their friends. Not only is this free time a time for enjoyment, but it is also a time when a number of basic skills are learned and developed. Indeed, in the opinion of Hall-of-Fame goaltender Ken Dryden, it is in this free time that special players, such as former star hockey player Guy Lafleur, develop, and not in the competitive environment of organized games. According to Dryden's calculations, a twelve-year-old boy playing a thirty-minute game is likely to see the ice for only about ten minutes. Dryden feels that this time might be better spent if the boy was allowed to play continuously on a backyard or playground rink by himself or with his friends without the encumbrances of the competitive setting.

Recreational Versus Competitive Sport

For a number of years now, a battle has been waged over the superiority of competitive versus recreational sports programs for children. For those of you who are not familiar with the differences between these two approaches, competitive leagues typically have extensive practice schedules, maintain league standing records, and culminate with post-season playoffs and a championship. Recreational leagues, while providing organized, structured competitions, typically have rotational playing time for all players regardless of ability, have limited practice times, do not publish league standings, and avoid all post-season competition.

Those who support competitive leagues suggest that participation in competitive sports increases the sense of discipline, encourages skill development, and promotes an understanding of the competitive process that will carry over into one's adult life. Critics of the competitive programs, on the other hand, suggest that this approach often undermines the psycho-social development of children because of the heavy emphasis placed on winning by parents and coaches.

The critics of the competitive programs are also quick to point out that the results of several different studies, using vastly different groups and measures of success, have shown that competitiveness is associated with poorer, rather than better performance. These critics have therefore suggested that children would be much better off if they participated in more recreational-type activities, where competition was de-emphasized and high quality participation, was emphasized.

Who is right? Which structure provides the best environment for the children? Unfortunately, there is little scientific evidence available at present that gives us a definitive answer to this question. However, the results of one recent study have provided some insight.

In this study, children participating in a competitive soccer program were compared to children participating in a recreational soccer program, using a number of important criteria, including reasons for participation, enjoyment, and attitudes (Scarisbrick & Allison, 1986). The results were very revealing.

The most interesting revelation was the fact that children in both programs had similar reasons for playing. Both rated having fun as the number one reason. Both groups felt very confident about their sporting endeavors and felt little anxiety about approaching a game situation. Furthermore, all of the children indicated that they wanted to return to the same program the following year.

But there were also some differences. For one thing, children in the competitive program tended to rate being a starting player on the team as much more important than the children in the recreational program did. The children in the recreational program much preferred playing regularly on a team that was not winning to playing on a winning team but having to sit out. The children in the competitive program rated themselves as much more highly competent in terms of skills than did the children in the recreational program.

These results suggest that neither approach is suitable for all children. Rather, it appears that both are valuable in their own right, because each serves different needs. The competitive league appears to be best suited for those children who want to improve their skills and compete, whereas those children who are interested in playing regularly in a low-pressure environment are likely to be better served in the recreational league. Different strokes for different folks.

The Dark Side

To conclude this chapter, I would like to issue one caveat to parents. Parents generally aspire to provide the best sporting experience for their children, but it does not always turn out that way.

Over the past few years, we have been studying the effects that parents have on a child's sporting experience. Unfortunately, the news has not always been good. In one study we conducted, coaches were asked to list the reasons why they might stop coaching. Parents ranked as the second most important factor!

In a second study, different coaches were asked to identify the reasons that might cause children to drop out of sport. According to these coaches, parents were again seen as the second most important factor. From a coach's perspective, parents are on the dark side of children's sport. The reasons for this negative perception, and the courses of action available to rectify it, are addressed in the forthcoming chapters.

Before we confront some of these issues, let us find out where you stand as a parent. The next chapter will help you determine your status as a sporting parent.

CHAPTER TWO

The Parenting Grid

"I like it when they ask how I did and share my pleasure and disappointment." *Female, 14, basketball*

Where do you stand as a "sporting parent?" To help you find out, think about how you would answer the following two questions about your child's sport involvement:

1. How important is it to *you* that your child strive to *win*?
2. How important is it to *you* that your child have *fun*?

Rate your responses using the following scale:
1 - not at all important
2 - somewhat important
3 - moderately important
4 - very important
5 - extremely important

Now, let us see where you are positioned on the Parenting Grid on the following page. Your response to each question determines your position. The responses at the bottom of the Grid represent how you feel about Question 1; the responses on the left represent your feelings about Question 2.

Here is an example of how the grid works. If you feel that it is

The Parenting Grid

Fun

	not at all important	somewhat important	moderately important	very important	extremely important
extremely important	C				A
very important					
moderately important		X			
somewhat important					
not at all important	D				B

not at all important · somewhat important · moderately important · very important · extremely important

Winning

"somewhat important" that your child strive to win in sport, and "moderately important" that your child have fun, your position on the Parenting Grid would be represented by the "X."

Now that you know where you stand, let's find out what it means by taking a closer look at the Parenting Grid. The Grid encapsulates what I feel are the two main ingredients in sport—winning and fun.

Winning

Although critics of sport often cite winning as one of the major factors contributing to a negative sports experience for children, it is also a very necessary part of sport.

To engage in sport without striving to win would be like going fishing and not trying to catch any fish. While there might be a reason for not wanting to catch any fish, the objective of fishing is still to catch fish. Similarly, in sport the objective is to win. To verify this, just look at a rule book from any sport. Each set of rules explicitly states that the objective of the sport is to score more goals, more points, or whatever.

Furthermore, it cannot be denied that winning is more satisfying than losing. In my experience, the feelings of excitement and satisfaction associated with playing well are enhanced by winning and diminished by losing.

But, from a realistic perspective, we can't always be winners. In any contest, there is always at least one loser. That is why the emphasis in sport should be on *striving* to win and not on winning itself. Note that Question 1 asked about "striving" to win and not just winning. This distinction was made deliberately: there is a very important difference between winning and striving to win.

This distinction is captured in the following quote from Margaret Lee Runbeck: "Happiness is not a station you arrive at, but a manner of travelling." Sport is no different. The satisfaction and enjoyment in sport come from the preparation, the challenges one faces, and the testing of one's abilities rather than from actually winning. Hence, the objective of the sport should be to strive to win rather than to win.

Children certainly recognize this distinction. For instance, sport psychologist Terry Orlick asked young hockey players what they preferred more—participating or winning. His results revealed that 90 percent of the boys questioned would rather play on a losing team than sit on the bench of a winning team.

Fun

From my perspective, the other major objective of sport should be fun—not an earth-shattering observation, perhaps, but an important one. If children are to benefit from sport, they need to stay involved and the surest way they'll stay involved is if they're having fun. Research into the motives of North American children involved in sport backs up this reasoning. When children were asked why they participated in organized sport, the first or second most important reason cited was always "fun" (Gill et al., 1983; Gould et al., 1986).

On the other end of the age continuum, older athletes often respond to questions about their impending retirement by saying that they will retire when the sport is no longer enjoyable. Trite as this may sound, it has been my experience that this emphasis on fun often truly and accurately describes these athlete's feelings.

In the words of ice-hockey great, Gordie Howe, "To me, hockey's always been tremendous fun. Maybe that's what keeps me going." When you think about it, it is not too surprising that fun holds such an important place in sport, because fun permeates most things we do, even the so-called "dog-eat-dog" world of business. Thomas Peters and Robert Waterman in their book *In Search of Excellence* made special note of the fact that the theme of fun in business ran through a large number of the excellent companies that they investigated. According to them, the leaders and managers in these excellent companies liked what they were doing and were very enthusiastic about it. In the words of Howard Head, inventor and entrepreneur, father of the Head ski and the Prince tennis racquet, "I just love design. If it weren't fun, I wouldn't do it." The same sentiment is echoed in sport. When asked to comment on the fact that he used to practice hockey four hours per night as a child, superstar Wayne Gretzky replied, "... looking back at it, I wasn't practicing. If I'd thought I was practicing I'd probably never have done it. I did it because that was what I had fun doing."

Having identified winning and fun as the two important factors in a rewarding sporting experience for children, let us now see how they interact. Returning to the Grid, you can see that each place on the Grid represents some degree of winning and some degree of fun. Although twenty-five different positions are possible, the Grid can be best explained by referring to the four corner positions—A, B, C, and D. The A position is where a good sporting parent would want to be. The following discussion explains why.

The A-parent

A number of decades ago, Grantland Rice conveyed the spirit of the Olympic Games when he suggested that it is not whether you win or lose but how you play the game that counts.

In today's success-driven world, most people pay little more than lip service to this thought. After all, how many people do you know who would regard the enjoyment of playing as an equal substitute for winning? The satisfaction and exhilaration associated with doing one's best is still heightened by winning and dampened by losing.

However, there is an important point here that is often missed by parents: winning and enjoyment of the contest are not mutually exclusive. In fact, they complement one another. Young athletes realize this. Their comments reveal that the most favored coaches are those who, "emphasize winning as well as fun," who "don't put winning ahead of fun," or who "believe in having fun as well as winning."

A-parents also understand quite clearly that the more their child enjoys and attributes importance to the contest itself, the more likely the child is to win. And conversely, the more the child wins, the more the contest will be enjoyed. Problems do arise when the two are kept apart. What a lot of parents fail to comprehend is that you can have fun while you're winning.

"They like me to win. When I lose they don't really care, but they still encourage me." *Female, 11, tennis*

The B-parent

The parent who occupies B on the Grid is one who sees outcome as the only value in sport. The basic problem here is that the B-parent often puts the sport first and the child second.

Let's put this type of parent into perspective. The B-parent is often depicted in the popular press as the "pushy" parent. I see them as Busy parents, hence their "B" designation on the Grid. The B-parent is the one who is always there providing the child with instructions on how to correct mistakes, handle an opponent, deal with the referee and so on. All of these instructions are intended to help the child to win because as far as B-parents are concerned, winning is the best thing for the child. When their children do not win, you are likely to hear them offer some disparaging remark: "Pity you didn't get that basket...score that goal...make that turn...stop that player...swim a little faster..."

In these situations, children need support, not a reminder that they have not done as well as desired.

Unfortunately B-parents tend to do more harm than good, even when their children have been successful. This process usually unfolds in the following manner.

It is a very normal part of the developmental process that children seek parental approval for their actions. However, this need for approval can cause problems if the child is being pressured by a parent with demands that are too high. When parents make unrealistic demands, children are continually frustrated because they can never please the parent.

You can usually identify B-parents by their constant demands for perfection. Even when the child has won an event, the B-parent is still pushing for improvements: "Your start was slow," "You straightened too quickly," "You let your opponent get too close," and so on.

What's wrong with this type of behavior? Certainly, the B-parent's intention, to help the child improve, is admirable. Furthermore, to obtain the perfect performance demanded by the parent requires preparation, continuous progress, and commitment—all characteristics associated with success. Undoubtedly, some elite competitors can attribute their later success to the high level of achievement demanded from them during their childhood.

However, in the quest for perfection for the child, the B-parent also exposes the child to a diet of continual failure. In short, no matter what the young athlete does or accomplishes, it is not good enough. Therefore, what B-parents perceive as encouragement is often interpreted by their children as evidence of failure.

"They say you should have done better even if you win." *Male, 14, hockey*

Although these demands may help the young athletes achieve in the short-term, over the long-term such demands result in inconsistent achievement and create difficulties in staying at the top, especially when challenged by an opponent of equal ability.

The C-parent

The "C" in C-parent stands for Comforting because these types of parents tend to want to comfort and protect their children from any bad experiences. C-parents are generally interested only in their child's welfare and enjoyment while eschewing the importance of outcome. For some people, this approach would be a welcome respite from the evils typically associated with a focus on winning. But, this is not always the case. In fact, it has been my experience that, from a child's perspective, this neutrality about whether the child wins or not often frustrates the child. Why should this be so?

It quite often happens that C-parents have a fear that if they become too involved with winning, they may become too "pushy." Consequently, they tend to err on the safe side, suggesting to their children that winning is not important. Vicki

Cardwell, a former Australian squash champion, who held eighteen national titles in seven countries, expressed this sentiment very clearly when she reported in a magazine article, "One of my concerns about myself is that I could be over-zealous if Joshua [her son] entered competitive sport."

Unfortunately, children often misinterpret this approach to winning to mean that their parents don't really care about their involvement in sport. For instance, when they are successful, they often wonder why their parents are not supporting them in their accomplishments.

"They don't seem very interested when I do well." *Female, 14, swimming*

Remember, we all need reinforcement. When a child has accomplished something, parents should show interest by sharing in the joy of that accomplishment.

"They are proud of me if I win." *Female, 10, gymnastics*

Now, do not misunderstand. C-parents are usually very good when things have not turned out as planned for the child. The main problem is that they do not provide enough reinforcement when the child has been successful.

"They never praise me whether I catch a pop fly or hit a grand slam." *Female, 14, baseball*

And, as we shall see in a later chapter, this support is often crucial for the development of a child, both on and off the playing field.

The D-parent

Parents who fall on D, or close to it, have what can be called a "babysitting" mentality. That is they generally treat sport for their children as simply a type of babysitting service. They are quite happy if sport, like a babysitter, occupies their child's time and then returns the child unharmed. They rarely show up at games or practices, and if they do, they take little interest in what their child is doing. At home, they rarely show any interest in whether the child is experiencing any success, or even enjoying the experience. D-parents come by their "D" name honestly, because they typically Do not care about their child's sporting life.

The main problem with D-parents is that they are involved too little with their child's sporting experience. Why is this a problem? Wanting parental approval is a normal part of child development: wanting approval and encouragement in sport is no exception.

"I like having my parents involved in what I do in swimming, and the support they give me." *Female, 14, swimming*

Children need to feel supported in whatever they do. Yet, too often, the child's sporting experience is relegated by the D-parent to the "not very important" category. This can have a very debilitating effect on children who like sport and recognize that it is highly valued by society.

"Mom doesn't take much interest at all in the sport. It would be good to have a bit more encouragement." *Male, 16, sailing*

The rule of thumb to follow here is best expressed by former ice hockey superstar Bobby Hull, who noted that "much of the success a boy enjoys at minor league sports can be measured by his parents' enthusiasm and interest."

What this book suggests is that the best sporting experience will be that of children whose parents understand that winning and fun are complementary goals of youth sport.

The chapters that follow outline some easy-to-implement guidelines to help parents create an environment in which their children will be able to realize their potential in sport and still enjoy the experience. Or, in the parlance of the Parenting Grid, you will be provided with suggestions that will move you toward being an A-parent. By the way, the "A" designation stands for a sporting parent who is A-O.K.

We shall start our journey by having a closer look at what must be one of the most discussed areas of children's sport—winning.

CHAPTER THREE

The Myth of Winning

"Sometimes they forget that you sometimes have a bad day."
Male, 17, swimming

"Everybody loves a winner." "There is no prize for second place." "Nice guys finish last." "Defeat is worse than death, because you have to live with defeat."

We've heard them all before—the testaments to the importance of winning. In our success-oriented society, it is not surprising that sport also adopts a philosophy that endorses the importance of winning. Most people who had an interest in the 1984 Olympics would likely remember that Carl Lewis won five gold medals. Very few of these same people, however would remember who finished second to him in any one of the five events.

There is no argument that winning is the rule-defined objective of sports. The sole purpose is to win by scoring more baskets, kicking more goals, scoring more points, or scoring more runs than your opponent. On the surface, the focus in sport should be obvious—WIN! Yet, ironically, it is the focus on winning that often makes winning difficult.

Watching the Pot Boil

What's wrong with focusing on winning? Nothing, if you win. Unfortunately, most of us sabotage our attempts to win by focusing on it. This paradox can be readily explained.

Whichever way you cut it, focusing on winning will not expedite our success. It's analogous to waiting for a pot to boil. As we all know, "A watched pot never boils." The more desperate we are that it boil quickly, the longer it seems to take. However, adjusting the heat or changing the amount of water in the pot will make it boil more quickly.

Sports are no different. Focusing on preparation makes much more sense than worrying about the outcome. Just as the pot will boil more quickly if the proper preparations are taken, so too the young athletes will be more likely to win if their preparation has been adequate.

Success is dependent upon preparation, not upon thinking or worrying about success.

Little Control

The problem is that winning is not under one's direct control. For instance, your son may have played his best tennis game ever, yet have been defeated by an opponent who has just played a slighter better version of *his* best game. The point is that a focus on outcome means that one has to compare favorably with other competitors. And, as any good competitor knows, there will always be a large number of factors associated with an opponent that are completely outside the athlete's control.

In children's sports, a number of unique factors associated with the developing child must also be considered. Some of these factors that are outside of the child's control are as follows.

Maturation Rates

You only have to look at any grade-school class to realize that children of the same age come in all shapes and sizes. It is a simple fact of life that children mature at different rates. Some children mature early, while others are slower to mature. In terms of the child's eventual development into an adult, there is likely to be little advantage in maturing early or late but, in sport, the structural, functional, and performance advantages of early-maturing children in sports requiring strength, power, and size are well-documented.

Think about it. What chance does a 13-year-old boy have of defeating an opponent who is forty centimeters taller and forty kilograms heavier than himself? Without bending the rules, the chances for success in any sport requiring strength, power, or size would be very limited.

This comparison may sound exaggerated, but it is certainly within the realm of possibility. It is well known that during puberty children experience widely divergent growth patterns. It is quite possible, for instance, that boys of the same chronological age may differ in their physical development by as much as five years.

This problem could be overcome, but the fact is that chronological age, and not size and weight, is often the sole criterion by which children are grouped together in a number of sporting activities. Children may therefore, often be put into sports situations where winning will be next to impossible. For a child whose most important goal is to win, this will create frustrations. It is little wonder then, that children often indicate that the greater strength, power and size of other children is one of the reasons why they drop out of sport.

It is also worth noting that the performance of some certain basic sports skills is controlled by growth rates. Children must reach certain levels of physical maturity before they can successfully execute certain skills. For instance, it is generally known that most children find it difficult to visually track a ball as it moves in an arc until they are eight or nine and a half years of age. Therefore, putting children under this age into little league baseball, for instance, where they must hit a pitched ball, makes it very difficult for them to enjoy success, and through no fault of their own.

That Clumsy Age

When a child experiences rapid growth spurts or changes in weight, there is often an initial period of clumsiness. Skills that were done well previously are now done with less proficiency. If the child is still expected to "win" during this period problems will arise. Although these children's skills are not as good as they were before, these children may still be expected to defeat opponents who have not been through a recent growth spurt and whose skills have, therefore, not lapsed.

Unfortunately, it is often happens that children who were "stars" at an earlier age receive little support during this period of "awkwardness." Quite often they are confronted with confused and frustrated parents who want to know why their child is not performing as well as before. Rather than being critical, parents should encourage the child to focus less on winning and to reduce performance expectations to a lower, more attainable level. Remember, the child has a new body shape, and different strength and flexibility characteristics. In all likelihood, many skills will have to be relearned. A focus on winning tends only to frustrate and confuse the child during the relearning periods.

Losing Teams

It is also possible that your children, through no fault of their own, may play in a team that always loses. No matter how hard they try, or even how skilled they are, they will not win because the team is not good enough.

Now, there is no problem with being on a losing team. There has to be a loser in every sport contest. The problem arises when the only reason for participating is to win. By stressing winning, you are putting the attainment of your children's goal beyond their control—not a very satisfying or envious position to be in.

While other reasons could be cited, such as differential rates in psychological or sociological development between children, it should be patently clear that winning a contest at any given point in time can often be beyond a child's control. Consequently, using outcome as the primary motivation for involvement in sport can be extremely detrimental to a child's enjoyment of, and ultimate participation in, sporting activities.

Besides the fact that outcome is often beyond our direct control, there are several other reasons why an outcome focus might result in failure. Included in this list are the following:

Ability Focus

Research has shown that individuals who are very outcome-oriented tend to focus on their ability. Outcome-oriented individuals judge their success on wins and losses, not on how they played. In one of my recent studies, I found that by changing the instructions to a group of athletes from "beat the other person" to "do your best and try to improve on your own performance," the athletes' focus changed from their ability to their effort. When they were told that the objective was to beat the other person, they tended to focus on their ability. When they won, they considered themselves skilled; and, when they lost they thought they were not very good. However, when the instructions were to improve their performance, their thoughts changed to effort and performance-related factors.

While this may seem like a rather harmless difference, the focus on ability that comes with an outcome orientation can cause severe problems, especially in individuals who see themselves as less than competent. Here is how it works.

When young athletes start to think about their ability, their thoughts often center on how they can demonstrate their ability. For those who have some doubts about how good they really are, and that includes a large number of children, this focus causes problems in the following areas:

Task Selection

Focusing on ability often influences the choice of tasks. If children hold a very high opinion of their ability, there is no problem. They will select tasks that challenge their ability. On the other hand, if children have some doubts about their ability, they will select tasks that conceal their real ability, or at least protect it from negative evaluation.

These young athletes will either tend to select tasks in which success is virtually guaranteed (i.e., very easy tasks), or to select very difficult tasks in which success is virtually impossible. For instance, a defensive back in football would likely either give his man a 5-yard cushion (a relatively easy task) or play in front of him hoping for an interception each time (a relatively difficult task).

Selection of either of these two types of tasks eliminates the possibility of the child making an unfavorable comparison with some other standard. The selection of an easy task is likely to result in a success, thereby eliminating the possibility of an unfavorable result. On the other hand, failure at an extremely difficult task can be easily rationalized with a statement such as, "None of the other children could do it either, therefore my failure is not that bad."

As you might expect, engaging in either very easy or very difficult tasks is not in the best interests of your child. If your child keeps selecting very easy tasks and accomplishing them, the accomplishment is a "hollow" one. The evidence from motivational research is very clear on this point: continued success at easy tasks is ineffective in producing a performer who will persist under more difficult conditions. On the other hand, the continual selection of extremely difficult tasks, and the failure that often ensues, will only serve to frustrate the child and may result in complete withdrawal from sport.

Consequently, it does not make much sense to foster an outcome orientation, with its attendant ability focus, in your child.

Persistence

Children who perceive winning as all important need a high opinion of their ability to sustain involvement in the sport. Unfortunately, it is often difficult for them to maintain this confidence because they interpret failures as signs of their lack of ability and view them as predictive of continued failure. This, in turn, often results in inadequate efforts when they next face a difficult challenge.

These individuals tend to think along the lines, "I'm not very good at this, so why bother really putting myself out? I'll only end up failing anyway." In other words, they feel a sense of helplessness. This translates into an attempt that is less than their best, which, in turn, is likely to increase their chances of failing. When they fail, they take this as another sign that they do not have the ability, thus perpetuating a downward spiral and possibly resulting in a complete withdrawal from sport.

Studies have revealed that individuals who drop out of sport are more likely to emphasize outcome goals (Ewing, 1981). That is, they tend to define their success and failure in sport more exclusively with respect to outcome: Did I win or did I lose?

Satisfaction

Individuals who focus on winning derive their satisfaction in sport from the ability they believe they have displayed. Unfortunately, they only feel they have displayed ability when they win. This is unfortunate, because not everyone can win.

From a mathematical perspective, the probability of two evenly matched athletes winning a contest is only 50 percent for each athlete. In the long-term, each athlete can expect to win approximately one half of the contests. If you are basing your satisfaction solely on winning, you are putting yourself into a very bad situation.

What happens if winning is your chidren's primary motivational goal, yet they are not the most skilled in the activity? What can they fall back on that will provide them with some feeling of success? Unfortunately, not much. Parents who stress, or allow their children to think, that success comes primarily through winning are not providing their children with much of an opportunity to be successful and, as a result, to feel good about themselves.

This is especially true for younger children just starting competitive sport because, in the initial stages, they will lack the requisite skills and strategies for mastering the game. For a great number of these children, winning will be very difficult. If success is equated with winning, the losers will not have many opportunities to feel good about themselves. Furthermore, because outcome is often outside of the children's control, there is little that children can do to change the situation.

So, if a focus on outcome is not the answer, what should the focus be?

Performance Factors

Up to this point, we have been talking about winning as an outcome goal. An outcome goal is simply a result. However, a number of factors contribute to every result. These factors are called *performance goals*—the means by which outcome goals are achieved.

How do you achieve the outcome goal of winning a running race? Since it is very obvious that the attainment of this goal requires that you cross the finish line first, it may seem superfluous to set any other goals other than to simply "go for it!" But, when you think about it, there are a number of things that have to be done in order to finish first. Some of these might include: getting a good start, maintaining good technique, controlling arousal, maintaining concentration, and adhering to a planned strategy.

A focus on performance factors rather than on outcome will enhance a child's rate of success. Research has revealed that male and female intercollegiate swimmers who received a performance-based, goal-setting program exerted higher effort and demonstrated greater performance improvements over the course of a season than did a control group of swimmers who focused more on outcome (Burton, 1985). A number of factors can help explain why a focus on performance results in greater gains than a focus on outcome.

For one thing, the attainment of an outcome goal (i.e., winning) requires that the child surpasses the performance of other children. This can create problems because a child is often not in a position, physically or psychologically, to defeat another child. The child may be a late maturer, may play on a poor team, or may be experiencing a growth spurt. Each of these factors works against the child's defeating an opponent.

Focusing on performance factors, on the other hand, circumvents this problem because performance factors have little or nothing to do with the opposition. Performance factors are under the control of the child.

This increased feeling of control often results in better performances because it fosters self-confidence. It is much easier to be confident approaching something that you know that you can control versus something over which you have little or no control.

For example, your children are likely to approach a tennis game with much more confidence if their goals are to get 60 percent of first serves in, hit 80 percent of their deep ground strokes to within one meter of the baseline, control their frustration after losing a long rally, control their temper after experiencing a bad line call, and so on, rather than if simply having winning as their goal. In the former situation, your children can control these performance goals, whereas the latter outcome goal involves a number of factors that your children cannot control. Their opponent's play on the day would be the most obvious of these.

There is also another problem with an outcome focus: uncertainty and anxiety. When we face a new challenge, there are always uncertainties present. In a sporting situation, these might include the uncertainty associated with how well the opponent will play, how the referees will influence the game, how the crowd will react to mistakes, and so on. Uncertainty leads to anxiety and anxiety often adversely affects performance.

However, this problem can be easily prevented if the children focus on performance goals. If performance goals for an event are familiar and clearly within the child's range of skills, then uncertainties and anxiety are significantly reduced, and performance enhanced.

Setting multiple performance goals allows children the opportunity to feel successful even in situations where winning is next to impossible. Thus, children who lose a swimming race could still feel successful if they had a good start, executed good turns, and finished well. However, if outcome is stressed as the primary goal of participation, the attainment of all of the performance goals will not result in any feeling of success.

The success that comes from the attainment of selected performance goals is positive feedback that enhances the child's self-confidence, even when the ultimate outcome has been a failure. Children who feel confident will look forward to entering sporting contests in the future, and that's the way it should be!

How to Measure Success

We all need to experience success. How will children know whether they have been successful if we take the importance of outcome away from them? The best criterion for success should be the attainment of selected performance goals.

What is the parent's role in this process? Parents can play a very important role in helping their children define and set specific, challenging, and realistic (i.e., attainable) goals. Note, the emphasis is on goals, in the plural. The more performance goals that are set, the more opportunities the child will have to be successful. For example, the following performance goals could be set for a young hockey player:
• Beat my man to the pack more times than he beats me.
• Make a break from my man each time our team gets the puck.
• Stay within a stride of my man when the opposition gets the puck.
• No offsides.
• Maintain pre-game arousal at a controllable level.
• Recover quickly from my mistakes, at least by the next shift.
• Concentrate for the full time that I am on the ice.
• Encourage teammates when I am on the bench.
If any of these goals are attained, then the child should feel successful. The more goals that are attained, the more successful

the child should feel. If all of the performance goals are attained, then the goals for the next game should be increased accordingly, either by improving on the last performance or adding new performance goals to the list.

You should not let your children become discouraged because they are not making improvements as fast as they think they should. Remind them that Roger Bannister, the first person to run a mile in less than four minutes, took six years to cut seconds off his time for the mile and a full year to cut the last two seconds off for his record-breaking accomplishment. All improvements, no matter how small, should be endorsed as successes building toward larger successes.

When helping your children set goals, it is important that you keep the goals specific. Specific goals are much easier for the child to attain. For example, the specific goal, "beat my man to the puck more times than he beats me," is much clearer in terms of what is required than is the more general goal, "work harder."

The goals also need to be realistic. "Realistic" in this instance means challenging, yet attainable. The goals should be based on realistic accomplishments rather than final perfection. Remember, no one is perfect and those who think that they are usually fall behind! Goals that are perceived by children as too high only serve to make them anxious.

The best way to avoid setting goals that are too high is to listen to what your children have to say. If the child provides the major input into the goals that are set, the likelihood of the goals being unrealistically high is minimized. Remember it is the child who has to perform, not the parent. It is more important that the goal appear realistic to the child than to the parent. And don't assume that siblings will develop the same skills at the same age. Realistic is in the eyes of the child.

So, there you have it—some thoughts on how to approach winning in a much more productive and fun way. Hopefully, you will now understand why outcome isn't the only thing in sport and why a focus on winning may often result in failure. If you want to become an A-parent, you will take the time to convey these ideas to your children. This will not guarantee that your children will always win, but it will reduce the number of times they fail. And, when they do fail, the next chapter will assist you in helping your children handle the defeat.

CHAPTER FOUR

Handling Defeat

"My parents treat me well at a soccer game, and if we lost they treat me like we won." *Male, 12, soccer*

In every sporting contest, there is going to be the "thrill of victory" and the "agony of defeat." And there can be little argument as to which of these two experiences is most desired. Most people, children and adults, like to win. But, as we all know, the cold reality of sport is that someone must lose.

While it's easy to be a good winner, it's much more difficult to face up to defeat. One of the greatest challenges that your child will face is to overcome failures and stay motivated to continue in the pursuit of greater sport goals. Handling defeat, in any venture or at any level, is never easy. Parents can play a very important role in helping their children handle the inevitable defeats that are inherent in any sporting contest. How? Some suggestions follow on how parents can help make those defeats palatable, yet productive for their children.

To Cry or Not to Cry

Failure in sport can be devastating to some children. Some young athletes can take failure in their stride, while others will carry a defeat for days and weeks. Here are some ways to help children recover from a loss more readily.

First, children who feel down after a contest should be allowed to express emotion, and that includes crying. B-parents, take note. Telling children who cry after a devastating defeat "not to act like a baby" is not appropriate. Even professional athletes sometimes shed a tear after losing important games. Sport is an emotional activity and the expression of emotion, whether one wins or loses, is natural. You wouldn't prevent your children from being excited and happy following a win, so why should you try to curtail their emotions after losing?

Keeping Losing in Perspective

When your children experience a particularly devastating loss, remind them that every athlete loses at one time or another— remind them that even the most successful athletes experience their fair share of failures. Remind them that Babe Ruth struck out more often than he hit home runs. People laughed at Roger Bannister's "unusual" running style until he recorded the world's first sub four-minute mile. Muhammad Ali lost the boxing heavyweight championship as many times as he won it (three). Up to 1987, the Dallas Cowboys have lost more Super Bowls than they have won. The list goes on.

Children need to know that they are not the only ones who lose in sport. While this may sound obvious, children who lose quite often think only of themselves. They cannot see the forest for the trees. The pain of defeat can be eased somewhat if someone important to them points out that even the "stars" lose their fair share of contests. Remind children that the very structure of sport produces more losers than winners. In a swimming meet, for instance, only one swimmer can have the best time, but that doesn't mean that the others had poor races.

Learn from Defeat

Children should be taught that a poor performance is not a failure if something is learned from the defeat. In fact, the only real way to improve ourselves is by correcting our mistakes.

Athletes realize this. A champion college football player once reflected that, "You don't learn anything when you win, but when you lose, you'd better." A similar feeling was echoed by basketball superstar "Magic" Johnson, who noted in a television interview that he never felt like a failure if he learned something from his mistakes.

Good athletes realize that to get better, one has to take risks and confront difficult challenges. They also realize that taking risks entails the possibility of mistakes and failures. But these mistakes and failures are a small price to pay for the satisfaction gained if success is achieved. Furthermore, good athletes generally believe that they will only get better if they allow themselves the right to make new mistakes. Mistakes to them mean they are pushing themselves to their limits, and this pushing is the key to improvement. You should ensure that your children understand this simple fact.

Rewarding the Attempt

Each time your children fail, you should go out of your way to reward their attempt. Why bother? After all, the contest is over, the outcome cannot be changed, the bad plays cannot be undone. The reason for bothering to reward the child's attempt has to do with something we call fear of failure.

As the examples of the well-known athletes noted above illustrate, no one athlete gets to the top without making many mistakes. Making mistakes does not hold these individuals back from achieving their goals. However, for others who do not make it, mistakes or, more specifically, the fear of making mistakes, impedes their improvement.

Why would children fear failure? Generally speaking, children who fear failure have a history of being criticized, belittled, and generally "put down" for their past mistakes: "Why didn't you do this?" "Why did you pass it there?" "That was a dumb thing to do." These are phrases that are heard all too often by a great number of children. A steady diet of this type of "put down" makes it inevitable that these children will start to fear failure. After all, who wants to put themselves into situations where they are likely to be criticized and maligned?

One simple suggestion to assist in reducing a child's fear of failure is to make sure that you reward all attempts, regardless of whether the result was a success or a failure. There is an important lesson here for parents. Before parents can feel comfortable enough to reward all attempts, they first must be able to accept their children whether they are "stars" or "bench warmers." In my estimation, this ability to accept one's children, regardless of their sports "status," should be a prerequisite for parents entering their children into sports for the first time.

Children who are praised for trying something, even though they may not have been successful, are more likely to want to try it again in the future.

"When I finish, if I came last they would say 'Good try, Danny.' *Male, 12, runner*

The more encouragement children receive for the attempt, the less likely they are to fear failure. And, the more attempts they make, the greater their opportunities to experience success. It's something to remember when your child needs some encouragement following a defeat.

The Silver Lining

We've all heard the old adage that "behind every cloud, there's a silver lining." Some people see this as simply a nice way of softening the blow of some misfortune, but it can be one of the most effective methods parents use to help their children handle defeat.

With few exceptions, there are positive aspects to failures. Unfortunately, these positive aspects are often overlooked because we tend to focus more on the bad parts of our performance. If we look closely enough, however, we will usually find that we have done something to feel good about.

Consider the case of the great Australian golfer Greg Norman. In the 1987 U.S. Masters, Norman lost on the second hole of a play-off when his opponent sank a great shot. When asked later about losing the tournament, Norman replied, "Well, at least I was there. As long as you get yourself into contention, you are there and are part of that history." Norman's comment suggests that he found something positive in a performance that some people might consider a failure. This approach to failure may be one of the things that makes Greg Norman a champion golfer.

But it may not be so easy for your children to find things to be positive about when they fail. That's where parents can help: they can act as a second set of "eyes," looking for things that their child has done well.

Take the example of a young tennis player who has just lost a match without winning a game in any of the sets. While the child is likely to have little trouble feeling miserable, the probability of the child seeing any good in the situation is minimal.

However, an observant parent may have witnessed that the child hit the backhand well, kept frustration under control, maintained relatively good court position, or played the net well. Any or all of these positive points could be brought to the child's attention. Once the child is aware that something positive did happen, it can only serve to enhance their confidence about tackling the next encounter.

But what should parents do if they cannot find something good in the performance? Should they still praise the child? Probably not.

Children, on the whole, prefer honest feedback. In fact, children who receive unwarranted positive feedback often become confused and even distrust its source. Parents who do this put themselves into a situation where their credibility will suffer in their child's eyes. Remember, you must praise only those things that deserve praise. If you cannot find anything positive in the performance, you're better off saying nothing!

"I don't like it when they see me play, and then when I loose they go, 'Don't worry.' " *Female, 11, gymnastics*

Minimize Criticism

When children lose, they generally feel bad. You do not need to tell them about it. Children generally accept criticism from coaches much better than they do from their parents. Parents do not need to become their children's coaches at home.

"I don't like it when you play a bad game and your parents criticize you." *Female, 12, tennis*

We will have more to say in a later chapter about this issue of the parent assuming an "unofficial" coaching role.

Having read this section, you know what A-parents know about the best ways to help you children handle defeat. You know that the best methods include keeping winning in perspective, assuring that your children learn from defeat, always rewarding your children's attempt, helping your children find the silver lining and keeping criticism to a minimum. Armed with this information, you will definitely be A-parent bound!

These last two chapters have established some ground rules concerning the parent's approach to winning and losing; the next chapter will look at success and failure from the child's perspective.

CHAPTER FIVE

You Are What You Think

"They clap when I do something good, and if I'm not playing well, they tell me to try harder." *Male, 14, baseball*

Do you know how your children explain their successes and failures on the sports field? Before answering that, you'll probably want to know why it's important that you do know. It's important because our thoughts about success and failure often affect the effort and persistence we devote to the same activity in the future.

Consider the case of Jill and her friend Sarah:

Both girls have been taking tennis lessons. True.

Both girls have been unable to master the one-handed backhand shot. True.

Both girls will persist in attempting to master this stroke. Maybe!

Why maybe? Well, before we can determine how the girls will react to their failure to master this stroke, we need to know something about how they explain their failures. When asked why she thinks she is having difficulty, Jill replies that she isn't applying herself enough and that she needs a little more practice. Sarah responds quite differently. She feels she is just not good enough to master the stroke. She has never been any good at racquet sports, so why should tennis be any different?

Although both girls have experienced the same difficulty, it would be safe to say, based on their explanations, that their subsequent behaviors will be much different. Jill will probably practice a little longer and a little harder until she masters the stroke. Sarah, on the other hand, may simply give up and forget about mastering the one-handed backhand.

Why the difference? To understand this, we need to have a closer look at how individuals explain their successes and failures. Psychologists have a name for these explanations of success and failure—they call them *attributions*. What attributions do your children make for their successes and failures? To find out, have your children do the following two exercises.

Exercise A

Ask your children to think about their favorite sporting activity. Have them think about a recent event in that sport that they regarded as a success. They may have won a game, scored a career high in points, or recorded a personal best.

Having identified a successful experience, ask them to list, on a sheet of blank paper, three reasons why they thought they were successful.

Exercise B

Using the same sport used in Exercise A, have your children think about a recent event that they regarded as a failure. They may have been defeated in a game, lost a club championship, or failed to make the finals.

Ask them to think about why they were not successful, and then list three reasons for that failure.

Now, let's find out what their explanations mean. To do this, we shall categorize the attributions as productive and debilitating. Attributions for success will be examined first.

Success

Productive Attributions

What are productive attributions? Since one of the major reasons to participate in sport is to feel good about oneself, productive attributions for success are those that allow an individual to take credit for things done well.

Productive attributions allow an individual to explain success using factors that reflect positively on the individual, factors that are internal to the individual, like skill and effort. For example, productive attributions for a tennis player might be something like:

1. I was successful today because I really applied myself throughout the entire match.

2. I was successful today because my first serve was powerful and accurate.

3. I was successful today because my selection of shots kept my opponent guessing.

Internal attributions such as these tend to elicit very strong feelings in an individual. For instance, you are likely to feel much more pride in a successful swimming race if you think that you won because you gave your best effort rather than if you think you won because your arch rival was sick.

Debilitating Attributions

Sometimes children deny personal responsibility for any of their successes. They do this by using explanations external to themselves. Continuing the tennis example, typical external attributions may include:

1. I was successful today because my opponent doesn't have a very strong backhand.

2. I was successful today because my opponent wasn't returning my first serve very well.

3. I was successful today because I got a couple of lucky shots to land on the lines.

Attributions such as these do not allow individuals to take credit for what they have accomplished. That's unfortunate, because we all need opportunities to feel good about ourselves. If we can't feel good about ourselves when we're successful, when can we?

Failure

Productive Attributions

Productive attributions following failure occur when individuals explain their failures using factors that they can not only control, but change. Productive attributions for failure in a tennis match would include things such as:

1. I didn't put in enough.
2. My shot selection was poor.
3. I didn't recover as quickly as I should have.

These are productive explanations for failure because they provide some hope that future outcomes will be different, since any of these factors can be changed prior to or during the next encounter. For instance, people who think, "I didn't put in enough," are implying that if they work a little harder next time, they will increase their chances of success. Jill's explanation for her failure to master the one-handed backhand shot fits into the productive category. It gives her hope that, with a little work, she will eventually master that particular stroke.

Debilitating Attributions

Debilitating explanations, on the other hand, are those such as:

1. My opponent was too good.
2. I got some bad line calls.
3. I got some unlucky bounces.

Why are these debilitating? They are debilitating because all of them are outside of the individual's control and offer no hope for success. In each of these explanations, external factors (i.e., the opponent, official's calls, and luck), not the individual's skills, abilities, or effort, will determine whether success is experienced in similar future situations. This is not a very envious position to be in, but a number of young athletes place themselves in it by not taking responsibility for their failures.

Explanations that suggest that failure occurred because of a lack of ability are also very debilitating. People who feel this often start to think like Sarah in her attempts to master the one-handed backhand. Like Sarah, they may start to feel helpless about achieving success because they believe they are simply not good enough. You can recognize their explanations following failure:

1. I'm too uncoordinated to learn this.
2. I'm just no good in sport.
3. I'll never be as good as Jim.

Individuals who explain their failures in this way usually lose interest in a sports task very quickly because they don't see any real reason to keep trying. As a result, they often put in very little effort and this results in further failure. Once this pattern is firmly entrenched, it is very difficult to feel optimistic about future success; the focus is almost exclusively on personal deficiencies.

As parents, it is very important that you realize that a strong relationship exists between how your children explain what happens to them on the sports field and their future behavior in the sporting arena.

Control

From what has been said thus far, it should be clear that success in sport is closely associated with the feeling of control. Athletes who feel in control of the situation are often the most motivated and the least anxious. They are also likely to be the most successful. To feel in control, athletes must assume responsibility for all that happens to them, including both success and failure. Unfortunately, for a number of young athletes, this is not as easy to do as it sounds. That's where parents come in. Here are some things that A-parents use to help their children assume more control of their sporting careers through the attributional explanations they use.

Smelling the Roses

The best attributions following success are those that allow your children to take credit for their success. If your children do take credit, you have little to worry about. Unfortunately, you cannot assume that they will. Often, young athletes explain their success using factors that are outside of their control.

They will, like the young tennis player, explain their success with statements such as, "My opponent wasn't hitting the ball well," "My opponent wasn't returning the serve well," or, "I got a couple of lucky breaks on the line calls." Explanations such as these do not allow the children to enjoy and feel good about their successes.

As a parent, you will be doing your children a big favor if you ensure that they do take responsibility for their triumphs. To do this, you need to know how your children explain their successes. The best ways to find this out are to ask them, and to listen to their answers.

If you find that your children are not taking any credit for their successes, you should look for things that will reflect positively on their ability. You will need to point out the connection between their performance and their ability. For instance, the attributions provided by the young tennis player could be turned to the child's advantage if the parent pointed out, "Your shot placement kept your opponent from hitting the ball well," "Your strong first serve minimized your opponent's return," and, "Your shot placement was excellent, allowing you to hit the lines on a number of occasions."

All of these explanations reinforce the connection between your children's success and ability. Quite simply, it gives them a chance to feel good about themselves, an opportunity that would have been missed if they believed in their original set of attributions!

Each time you help your children make this connection between their success and their ability, you are providing them with one more opportunity to "smell the roses"—to sit back and bask in the glory of their accomplishment. Too many times in life, we let accomplishments go unheralded. That's unfortunate. When something is done well, it should not go unnoticed.

You should also be aware that a number of research studies have found that children who drop out of sport often cite reasons that relate to their perceived poor ability. For instance, one study conducted with young wrestlers revealed that those who had dropped out took little credit for any of their wrestling successes (Burton & Martens, 1986). Sometimes, children need to be helped to see that they do have some ability.

"They cheer me on and congratulate me when I do something good." *Male, 12, basketball*

Remember, your children will not always make the obvious connection between their skill and abilities and success. Sometimes, it takes someone else to point this out to them. This sentiment was captured very clearly by Hubert Armstrong, the father of 1984 Olympic Games gold medalist Debbie Armstrong (giant slalom), who once revealed, "Debbie once told me, 'You can be great, but you have to hear it.' "

Taking Control of Failure

Parents should also be aware of how their children explain their failures. As with success, it is important that children assume responsibility for their failures. If you hear your children explaining their failures by citing bad luck, the weather, bad breaks, or poor officiating, you know that they are not taking control. They are relying on factors outside of their control, not on their own abilities and effort, to determine their destiny. As you would expect, children in this situation will not confront future contests from a position of strength.

There is also a message for C-parents here. C-parents often protect their children by attributing their failures to outside factors. The children themselves are never faulted because their parents always find some external reason for the failure. Some of the more common explanations from parents include, "You're teammates played poorly," "The coach made a bad decision," "You were unlucky," and so on.

The problem with these explanations is that the children may come to believe that the causes of what happens to them are beyond their control. As a result, children may lose sight of the fact that they must take responsibility for their own behaviors.

Another attributional pattern that parents should be on the lookout for is exhibited by the child who thinks failure is due to a lack of ability, just like Sarah, our young tennis player. Children who think this come to believe that they are helpless to change anything for the better because they are not good enough.

Parents should encourage children to perceive failure as being due to factors that they can not only control, but also change. "Not training enough," "Use of inappropriate strategies," "Not controlling frustration well enough," "Not enough concentration" are all good explanations for failure because they provide your children with some hope that the future will be better if they improve and/or change these factors.

"When I lose they encourage me to try harder." *Female, 12, swimming*

A caveat is also in order regarding the attributions that parents encourage. It is imperative that the explanation be realistic. For instance, telling children who are trying their best that they have failed because they have not tried hard enough is likely to backfire.

There is a special message here for parents who have children under the age of ten. Psychologist John Nicholls has found that children under ten explain most of their outcomes in terms of effort or lack of it. The message for parents of these young children is that "not trying enough" is not a good attribution to promote following failure. Remember, the explanation must be one that the child can act on with the possibility of improving their chances of success.

In summary, to be an A-parent you need to be not only aware of how your children perform, but also of how they explain these performances. As we have indicated, these explanations greatly influence the children's future motivation and behavior. A-parents listen and question and, as a result, are likely to be in a much better position to help their children enjoy their sporting experience by ensuring that they take responsibility for the outcomes they experience.

Speaking of enjoyment, one of the things that almost universally detracts from children's enjoyment of their sport is anxiety. When children become overly anxious, both their enjoyment and performance suffer. The next chapter examines why children might become anxious while participating in sport and what can be done about it.

CHAPTER SIX

Shaking All Over

"Having my dad watch can be a drawback because he puts too much pressure on you to be perfect." *Male, 14, hockey*

One of the crosses that youth sport has had to bear over the years is the criticism that it is excessively anxiety-producing for the participants. Critics of youth sport are more than willing to parade examples of the detrimental effects of anxiety on the children involved. There are the stories about young Jimmy who was physically sick with worry before the National Championship, or twelve-year-old Paul who became so anxious before his first regional final that he literally froze in the starting blocks, or Sally who wouldn't eat for two days after the local finals because she was so upset about losing.

While these are all very real and serious examples of the negative effects of anxiety on youth sport participants, before we make our final judgment on whether sport produces too much anxiety, we should probably find out if these examples are the exceptions or the rule.

How Stressful Is Sport?

Is the competitive sport setting environment creating a generation of stressed-out kids, as the critics suggest? Or, are isolated examples giving us a distorted view of the situation? From the research available, it appears that the latter suggestion is closer to the truth. (Please note that the terms *anxiety* and *stress* are used interchangeably throughout this section. In reality, there are distinctions between these terms: the interested reader can find these outlined in Martens's, *Sport Competition Anxiety Test*.)

Several years ago, two sports psychologists, Dr. Simons and Dr. Martens, set out to determine how stressful competitive sports actually were for the participants. To put this into perspective, they also measured how anxious children became in other traditional evaluative settings, such as taking a test in school, participating in physical education activities, and competing in musical competitions, either as soloists or as members of a school band.

The results from the testing of over seven hundred children revealed that the anxiety suffered in sports situations was not excessive, and was, in fact, no worse than that experienced when taking academic tests or performing in the school band. Interestingly, sport did not even rank first in terms of producing the greatest levels of anxiety. Music solos held that "honor." So much for singling out sport as the greatest source of anxiety for children!

Based on evidence such as this, it seems that, on average, children participating in sport are not exposed to excessive levels of anxiety. But, on the other hand, no child is average. Certain children in certain situations *will* experience excessive anxiety.

Fingerprints

Just as no two fingerprints are alike, no two children are exactly alike in the way they cope with stress. It is an accepted fact that some children are simply less stress-resistant than others. Some children can cope relatively easily with extraordinary problems, such as the death of a loved one, whereas other children have problems dealing with ordinary life stresses, such as the breaking of a favorite toy. Why do these differences exist? As you might suspect, there is no simple answer to this question. It appears, however, that the significant difference in a child's ability to cope with varying levels of stress is attributable to such things as the child's personality, intelligence, optimism, and resilience.

Competitive Anxiety

In the sports setting, a similar picture emerges. The only difference is that, in sport, we give anxiety a special name—sports competition anxiety. According to sports psychologist Rainer Martens, who identified and developed the term, competitive anxiety is an individual's fear response to competing in sporting contests.

Similar to the individual differences that emerge in dealing with everyday stresses, there are also differences in the way that individuals respond to the stress of sporting situations. As a result some children will be more anxious than others when they participate in a sporting contest. To understand why this occurs, we need to be aware of the difference between objective and subjective stress.

The Eye of the Beholder

In sport, as in life, there is often a difference between what is happening—the objective situation—and what the person perceives is happening—the subjective situation. And, not too surprisingly, it is the person's perception of the situation that determines what that person will do. It is no different with stress. For all intents and purposes, stress is created by what is in the eye of the beholder.

For example, moving from their hometown can be quite stressful for some children, yet others may perceive it as an exciting opportunity. A similar picture emerges on the sports field. The need to change positions on a team may be extremely stressful for one child, but, for another, each change may be seen as opportunity to learn new skills.

There are two points worth noting here, especially for B-parents. First, what parents consider to be a reasonable request in terms of a child's participation may not always be perceived that way by the child. For instance, based on your child's past record of successes, you may be quite realistic in stating that your child will have no difficulty defeating a known opponent. On the surface, there is no real reason for your child to be anxious facing this opponent because he has defeated this person many times before.

Objectively, this is sound reasoning. However, if your child's perception of the situation is different, then it is quite possible that the situation may be perceived as being more stressful. It may be that your child is going through a period of poor play and, as a result, may hold a great fear of losing to a "lesser" opponent. Although it is "realistic" to expect your child not to worry, it is your child's perception, not yours, that determines how stressful the sporting situation is. Unfortunately, when a discrepancy arises, parents often inadvertently force their perceptions on the child, making the situation seem even more stressful for the child.

A second point worth considering is the fact that, because of individual differences in competitive anxiety, it is quite possible that two children will respond to the same sport situation with very different anxiety levels. Entering a final, for instance, may cause one child to feel excessively anxious, while another may approach the game with a much lower and more controllable level of anxiety.

Individuals who are high in competitive anxiety perceive more things in the sporting situation as threatening and, as a result, become more anxious. As they approach a final, they may perceive a discrepancy between their ability to perform and the standard of skill perceived as necessary for success. In other words, they may think that they are not good enough to be successful and, as a result, feel very anxious about performing.

Individuals who are low in competitive anxiety, on the other hand, perceive far fewer things as threatening in the sport setting. As they approach a final, their thoughts are likely to be focused on how capable and confident they are. Such thoughts generally result in an anxiety level that is more appropriate and manageable.

You can probably get a fairly good indication of your children's level of competitive anxiety by finding out how they usually feel before participating in sporting contests.

Do they feel uptight, nervous, queasy? Do they worry about making mistakes, or about how they will perform? If your child experiences these feelings and thoughts before most sporting contests, then your child is probably high in competitive anxiety. If, on the other hand, these feelings and thoughts are experienced less frequently, then your child is probably low in competitive anxiety.

By knowing the level of your children's competitive anxiety, you will be in a much better position to understand how anxious they will become in a specific sporting situation. Let us imagine that you have two sons who are playing on a team that is about to enter the city final. Furthermore, you know that one of the boys is high in competitive anxiety, while the other is relatively low. Based on what you have read thus far, you would expect that these two boys will approach this final with different levels of anxiety.

The child who is low in competitive anxiety will approach the game in a relative state of calm, whereas the other child will likely get "wound up" and experience an excessive level of anxiety that will not only be unpleasant, but will also impair his performance. Their parents should treat these two boys differently as they approach the game.

What can you do? What follows is a list of factors that tend to generate anxiety in people generally, and in athletes specifically. By identifying these factors and outlining where parents can help, it is hoped that you, like A-parents, will be in a better position to assist your children to keep their anxiety at a reasonable and manageable level.

Pleasing the Folks

First things first. Children have identified parents as one of several pre-game factors that influence their anxiety levels. Research on children involved in competitive wrestling, for example, revealed that those children who felt that they had to wrestle to please their parents were much more likely to experience stress than those who do not feel such parental pressures (Scanlan & Lewthwaite, 1982). Are you pressuring your children to participate in certain sports? In terms of the anxiety that you might be generating, it would pay to find out.

"I don't like karate very much but I have to go because mom forces me into it." *Female, 10, karate*

Winner Take All

Not surprisingly, the need to win is often associated with increased stress levels. Actually, it is not the need to win, per se, but rather the uncertainty of the outcome that creates the problems. After all, if there was no uncertainty about winning, there would be no need to feel anxious. It's not the winning that is important here, but rather the concern that one might lose. Research has clearly illustrated that those who lose experience higher levels of stress than those who win.

Where do parents fit in? After all, parents don't make children lose. Why should they be implicated in this situation? It's quite simple really. The young athletes who experience heightened levels of anxiety as a result of losing, have, most likely, been strongly influenced by the adults in their lives to believe that winning is desirable and good, while losing is bad and shameful.

Parents often define their own worth in terms of their children's success. While it is quite natural for parents to identify with their children and want them to do well, some parents go too far and end up living their lives through their children. When this occurs, the parents become "winners" and "losers" based on their children's performances. Children in this situation often feel excessive pressure to win.

It also needs to be made clear that losing is not all that bad or shameful. Even sports greats lose their fair share of events. Consider the great baseball player Babe Ruth. Most people know that he was a prolific hitter who held the record for home runs in a single season. But, how many people know that during the same season he held the record for home runs, he also held the record for strike-outs? Not too many, I would imagine.

Not only do champion athletes experience their share of failures, they also accept them for what they are—learning experiences. Unfortunately, most adults react very negatively to failure; yet failure is a natural part of getting better. This can be difficult for children to understand if the adults in their lives make winning the *sine qua non* of sport. Babe Ruth could learn from failure, and he was a champion. When asked about the negative aspects of striking out so often, Ruth replied that he didn't mind striking out because every time he struck out, he knew he was one strike closer to another home run.

While Ruth understood that there was no real problem with striking out, do you? Do you let your children know that failure isn't such a bad thing and, in fact, that it can be beneficial if something is learned from it? Or, do you give them the idea that winning is the most important thing, that there is little consolation in finishing second? Do you even know what emphasis you convey? Let's have a closer look at how an emphasis on winning might be communicated.

The Sledge Hammer

Children learn in some very obvious way that winning is to be cherished and losing is to be feared. If your children see you always showing their latest trophy to the neighbors, bragging about them to your friends, berating opposition players and officials, or only see you turning up when they are doing well, they will readily believe that "everyone loves a winner," even parents.

"I don't like it when they start bragging about me." *Male, 14, swimming*

"They're always bragging about me, it's so embarrassing." *Female, 14, tennis*

"I don't like when they talk about me when I'm out of earshot —about my abilities and disabilities—because that embarrasses me!" *Female, 14, basketball*

Are you keeping winning in perspective?

The Subtle Approach

In addition to these obvious examples, there are also more subtle ways in which parents convey to their children that winning is the only thing. If you answer *yes* to a majority of the following questions, your children will probably think that winning is the only important goal in sport.

• Do you ask your children who won before you ask them how they played?

I like it when they don't ask me if I won." *Male, 14, rowing*

• Are you continually looking for ways to improve your child's chances of success?

"I do not like it when I lose a set or game and they tell me what I should have done." *Male, 14, tennis*

"When I lose they say, 'You lost. I told you should have done what I said.' " *Male, 12, tennis*

• Does your behavior toward your child differ following a failure versus after a success?

"I hate it when I lose because dad always gets so quiet in the car." *Male, 14, swimming*

• Are you constantly inquiring into how your child's skills are progressing?

"My dad's always asking the coach how I can get better—Yuk." *Female, 13, diving*

• Are you always comparing your child's skills to those of other children involved in the same sport?

"They forget you can't always break times, or they might want you to beat someone because they don't like them." *Male, 17, swimming*

How did you fare? If you answered *yes* to a majority of these questions, then your children may be suffering unduly from the stresses associated with seeing winning as the only acceptable outcome in a sporting contest. Remember, children learn the meaning of sport from the important adults in their lives.

Now, what's to be done? The most important thing that parents can do is to play down the importance of outcome. Winning is certainly important, but it is more important that your children recognize that there are equally important goals in sport, such as doing one's best. Any parent who emphasizes always trying hard and doing one's best will never have to fear that their child will suffer from excessive stress. When children realize that there is no shame in losing if they have done their best, they will fare very well in the "stress-free" stakes. Furthermore, the more they focus on the performance factors that they can control, the more likely they are to win!

"Sometimes they come and support me, and they don't worry if I do well or not, they only like me to try. I get support in whatever I do." *Female, 14, gymnastics*

"He accepts it when I lose or don't play well." *Female, 16, tennis*

"They encourage me to play to my best level." *Male, 17, baseball*

Stressful Thoughts

Consider the following scenario. As you wait to take a test, give a speech, or perform something in public, you start to think about how you will fare. If your thoughts are framed in terms of questions, such as, "Will I be able to pull it off?" "Will I be able to answer all of the questions?" or, "Will I remember all of my key points?" then you will start feeling somewhat anxious. This is not a pleasant feeling and does little to engender confidence as you wait to start.

Children have similar thoughts. The anxiety levels experienced by young athletes are often influenced by their thoughts as they approach a game or meet. Children who harbor thoughts about failure before they enter a sporting contest often experience much greater stress levels than those who do not have such thoughts.

What can parents do to help? As a parent, you can't control your children's thoughts. Or, can you? Although you can't control what your children actually think as they enter a sporting event, the things that you emphasize will have some influence on what your children think.

One of the most important things that A-parents emphasize is the factors that their children can control.

That means forgetting about talking outcome. What may appear to you as a useful "pre-game" talk may, in fact, be causing increased anxiety in your child. For instance, what you think is a reassuring statement, such as, "I know you're going to win today." may simply get the child to focus on outcome and, as a result, make the child feel more anxious. But, stressing that children do their best is not nearly as anxiety producing, because this is something they can control.

"I hate it when my dad says I will win. I might let him down." *Male, 15, hockey*

"They help me to do my best in sport." *Male, 12, baseball*

To do their best, children should be taught to think about all of the factors that they can control. For example, young swimmers could be encouraged to focus on their starting technique, race strategy, turning requirements, or stroke mechanics, rather than on whether they will win or lose the race. Parents who ask their children about performance factors will probably get their children thinking about these factors too.

After the Final Siren

Parents can also influence their children's thoughts following an event. Although the event ends with the final siren, the thinking about the event does not usually stop then. Parents can have a very large impact on how their children will approach future sporting contests, including what they will think about, during this post-game period. To a very large extent, what parents say following an event reveals to young athletes what is important to their parents.

What do you say to your children when they return home from some sporting contest? If you're a B-parent, your first question might be, "Who won?" This sounds like a rather innocuous question. In fact, it may even be a good question, if you're a C-parent, because you're showing some interest in your child. However, let's have a look at this question from the child's perspective.

More often than not, the question, "Who won?" conveys to children that winning is the only thing to be valued in sport. Each time you ask your children who won, you may be reinforcing the importance of outcome in their minds. There is no problem in emphasizing outcome if the children are going to experience "winning" consistently; but for most children, that won't be the case.

A much better approach—one followed by A-parents—is to have your children think about their performance as well as the outcome. How do you do this? By simply asking your children questions about relevant performance factors.

If your child is involved in tennis, you might ask questions that include any or all of the following:

How did you hit your groundstrokes?
How were your baseline shots today?
How well did you volley?

Were you getting good pace on your second serves?
How consistent was your return of serve?
Did you warm-up properly?
Did you play out the entire match?
Were you able to control your emotions on the court?
How quickly did you recover from your mistakes?

Questions such as these get children to think about factors that they control, which will put them into a much better position in terms of the "stress" stakes.

You Played Well, But

Negative feedback from parents also causes children to feel anxious. If children receive a more or less continuous diet of negative feedback, they start to worry about being negatively evaluated, even before the contest starts.

B-parents who are constantly "helping" their children to improve are often the most guilty of making their children worry about being evaluated negatively.

"Sometimes they encourage me so much that they get really angry if I'm not playing to my best ability." *Female, 13, volleyball*

With the noblest of intentions, some parents, who want to help their children improve themselves, identify faults to be corrected. There can be no argument that the best way to improve is to identify problems and correct them. But unfortunately, continually finding faults quite often leaves children frustrated and anxious. They feel they can never fully please the parent. This can be particularly devastating when the children experience what they consider a success:

You had a good race, but your start needs work.

You won easily, but your second serve needs more pace.

The win was good, but your turns were too slow.

You scored three goals, but your passing needs to be improved.

Although each of these comments acknowledges that something good has been done, each one is qualified by a "but" statement that may suggest to the child that parental approval is not complete. Since parental approval is extremely important to children, they often interpret these qualifying statements to mean that they are not "complete" successes in their parents' eyes.

This can be very damaging to a child's self-esteem, especially when the child has done everything humanly possible to please the parent.

"They hardly praise me. All they ever do is find my little mistakes and then they give me a lecture on them, even if I know what I'm doing wrong." *Female, 16, tennis*

To illustrate this point further, consider the case of former Oriole pitcher Mike Flanagan, who once struck out thirty-one batters and walked only one in a high-school baseball game. Flanagan thought that his father would finally tell him how well he had done, but this was not to be. What his father said was, "How come you walked that guy?"

You might remember this the next time you're praising your child for a job well done. Do you really need to qualify your praise? For the sake of the child, I hope not. You wouldn't withhold love from your child, then why withhold unqualified praise? It is certainly something to think about.

So, in summary, how do you keep your children from "shaking all over?" If you're like an A-parent, you will ensure that you don't put pressure on your children to participate in a sport that you like, but they do not; you will emphasize performance factors as well as outcome; and you will give "unqualified" praise for performances that are well done. By following these suggestions, your children should experience less anxiety and enjoy their sport more.

The suggestion in this chapter that children may feel pressure to participate in sports to satisfy the demands of their parents begs the even larger question of why children participate in sport in the first place. That is the next chapter.

CHAPTER SEVEN
To Play or Not to Play

"They give me money when I score goals." *Male, 13, hockey*

What do you know about your children's involvement in sport? If you're like most parents, you probably know how far they can jump, how many points they are likely to score in a basketball game, how quickly they can swim a race, or how likely they are to serve aces in tennis. While most parents know their child's "output," they generally know much less about the "input." about what their children think about their sporting experiences.

How important is it to know what your children think about their experiences in sport? Very important. This can be illustrated by looking at children's motives for participating in sport.

Motives for Participation

One of the first things that A-parents are interested in finding out is why their children are involved in sport. For some of you this might seem like a rather academic question. After all, your children are already in sport, they train regularly, and they participate in the games, so why worry about their reasons for participation? A good question, especially for those of us who believe in the old adage "If it's not broken, why fix it?" But, there is another side to the coin—why wait for something to break before we do something? The wisdom of this is illustrated in the following example.

Jack and Jill

Jack and Jill are the children of Mr. and Mrs. Sporting Parents. Jack and Jill are involved in swimming. Superficially, there appears to be very little difference in their involvement. They train at the same pool, at the same time, under the same coach, and swim in the same meets. Furthermore, their swimming accomplishments thus far are very similar. Both have won local championships for their age group.

But their reasons for participating are very different. Jack is two years older than Jill and, consequently his "gift" as a swimmer was noted by his parents first. They saw his potential as a swimmer and have done everything in their power to give him the best opportunity to develop. Each time he wins a championship, they reward him with "little perks," such as an increase in allowance, a visit to a favorite park, or a new bicycle.

Jack's parents also "help" him out when he doesn't feel like training. They realize that Jack will only get better if he trains hard. Therefore, each time Jack shows any inclination toward not training, his parents threaten him with some type of punishment, such as the temporary withdrawal of his allowance, the restriction of his television privileges, or a curtailing of his social life.

Jill, on the other hand, is in a very different situation. While she receives encouragement and support for her swimming, her parents do not reward her for her achievements, except for words of congratulations, nor do they threaten her with parental punishment if she is not training hard enough. Now, don't misunderstand, Jill's parents love her and want her to do as well as Jack. Their reticence to reward or punish her in the swimming realm merely reflects the fact that they think she is still very young and that she is also good at lots of other things anyway, including school and drama.

The question now arises: Since they are both achieving success in swimming, does it really matter what their motivations are? The answer, probably, is *yes*.

Jack's motivation, to all intents and purposes, is coming through his parents. Psychologists call this external control and I like to use a marionette analogy to illustrate what this means.

As we all know, a marionette is a small puppet, with jointed limbs, that moves only when someone manipulates the attached strings or wires. The marionette is under external control.

The same thing can happen with children. Young athletes who are rewarded for accomplishments or punished for failures are being manipulated by an external source. A parent is "pulling their strings" to make them perform. And perform they do. Most of us know children who pick themselves up and become really motivated when promised a reward or threatened with some type of punishment. The promise of an ice-cream for cleaning up the yard can do wonders for a child's motivation.

But, there are some problems with this "pulling of strings," the major one being that the parent, rather than the child, is providing the motivation. If the child starts to rely on the parents for motivation, then the parents must always be there to do the motivating.

Consider what happens when the parents are not there to pull the strings (maybe because they lose interest in the child's progress, or they don't have enough time). Or consider what happens when they can't pull the strings hard enough (maybe, over time the rewards and punishments lose their effectiveness). In both cases, interest and motivation decline. In their puppet-like state, these children depend on their parents for motivation and their self-motivation is non-existent. This is probably true for Jack.

Jill, however, is not being manipulated. Rather, she is generating her own motivation. In psychological parlance, she is intrinsically motivated. People who are intrinsically motivated do not do a task to receive a reward or avoid a punishment. They, like Jill, do something because they get enjoyment out of trying to master a skill.

Jill, like most of the kids we test, participates in sport for intrinsic reasons. Children tell us they like to learn new skills, they like the thrill of competing, they like the challenges involved in sport, they like to do something they are good at, and they just like to have fun—all intrinsic reasons. Children who are intrinsically motivated have no need to receive an external stimulus from someone else to get them going. Jill was motivated to achieve something in swimming, even without her parents standing over her. Jill is self-motivated, and that's the way it should be.

What would happen if Jill's parents started to give her monetary rewards for her accomplishments? Before addressing this question, it is worth noting that this is of more than academic interest. One finding of the recent *Miller Lite Report* on American attitudes toward sports was that 40 percent of all parents gave their children special treats or privileges for winning a sporting event.

If a Little Is Good ...

By giving an additional incentive to Jill's already high interest, one might logically expect that Jill would be even more motivated. After all, if a little motivation is good, a lot has to be better. This sounds good in theory, but it doesn't always work in practice. In fact, several studies have clearly demonstrated that external rewards not only do not enhance an individual's initial interest in an activity, but also often tend to undermine or decrease intrinsic motivation in sport and motor tasks (Halliwell, 1978; Orlick & Mosher, 1978).

According to Dr. Edward Deci, one of the eminent authorities in the area of intrinsic motivation, this occurs in one of two ways. One way in which an individual's motivation can be decreased is when the reward offered starts to control the individual. Rather than doing the activity for intrinsic reasons, the individual is motivated to do the activity for external rewards. Take our example of Jack. If his parents are there to reward him for his performance, he is motivated to continue. If they are not present for some reason, then his motivation is likely to decline. The following story illustrates how a reward can start to control an individual's behavior.

An old man lived alone on a street where boys played noisily every afternoon. One day the din became too much, and he called the boys into his house. He told them he liked to listen to them play, but his hearing was failing and he could no longer hear their games. He asked them to come around each day and play noisily in front of his house. If they did, he would give them each a quarter. The youngsters raced back the following day, and made a tremendous racket in front of the house. The old man paid them, and asked them to return the next day. Again, they made noise, and again the old man paid them for it. But this time he gave each boy only twenty cents, explaining that he was running out of money. On the following day, they got only fifteen cents each.

Furthermore, the old man told them, he would have to reduce the fee to five cents on the fourth day. The boys became angry, and told the old man they would not be back. It was not worth the effort, they said, to make noise for only five cents a day (Casady, 1974, p.52).

In the same way, by providing your children with rewards for a sporting activity that they already enjoy, you run the risk of shifting their motivation for participation to some outside factor. When this occurs, they start to rely on the reward for motivation. When that reward is no longer there or unattainable, they, not surprisingly, lose their motivation to participate. Consider what you would do if the company you worked for either reduced your pay or stopped paying you. Why should children be any different?

Keep in mind that this decrease in motivation only occurs when the child already has an interest in the activity (i.e., is intrinsically motivated). Obviously, rewards cannot decrease intrinsic motivation if no initial interest exists. In fact, parents can feel quite safe in rewarding their children if they participate in new sporting activities. However, once the children start to feel a sense of competence and natural interest starts to develop, rewards should be phased out.

Rewards inform individuals about their competence. For example, receiving a gold medal for placing first in the Olympics provides positive information that enhances an individual's feeling of competence. Receiving such positive feedback is likely to increase our intrinsic motivation.

However, the informational component of a reward is like a two-edged sword—it cuts both ways. To receive positive information about competence, one needs to get the reward. Children who strive for, but fail to attain, a standard where they would receive a reward may receive negative information that undermines their feelings of competence. In this situation, intrinsic motivation is likely to be undermined. After all, who likes to keep doing an activity when the feedback suggests that one is no good?

As previously noted, winning can often be a very difficult goal for a child to attain because there are so many factors that cannot be controlled. Therefore, it would not be very wise for parents to offer rewards to their children for games won, titles captured, or championships gained because, more often than not, the child will be unable to attain the desired outcome. Consequently, not receiving the reward becomes a form of negative feedback that decreases feelings of competence and intrinsic motivation.

A Better Approach

What types of rewards can parents offer that will provide their children with positive information about their competence? Rewards for the attainment of certain performance goals would be more appropriate. Parents who reward their children for the attainment of clearly specified performance goals (e.g., finishing strongly, controlling frustrations, playing their position well) that are perceived by the children as being within their reach are likely to provide them with the needed competence information. This type of reward will increase, rather than undermine, the children's interest and motivation in the activity.

The preceding discussion pointed out how rewards can affect your child's motivation. The major point is the child's *interpretation* of the reward is what is critical. If the reward is perceived by the child as controlling their performance or if it detracts from the child's feelings of competence, intrinsic motivation will decrease, whereas rewards that increase feelings of competence and control will increase motivation. Therefore, to ensure that Jack and Jill stay motivated for the right reasons (i.e., intrinsic reasons), it is imperative to understand their reasons for participation and how they are motivated. Offering a big reward or carrying a big stick are not always the best approaches!

A-parents realize that the best type of motivation is one that comes from the child. Children who develop a natural interest in sport, who like to learn new skills, who like to be challenged, who like to do something that they are good at, and who have fun doing it are "pulling their own strings" and need no additional "motivation." As an A-parent, you should understand this critical difference between intrinsic and extrinsic motivation and use this information to enhance your children's motivation to participate in sport.

Knowing why your children are participating in sport is very important, but it is equally important that parents consider what they expect their children to get out of sport. As the next chapter reveals, the expectations of parents often play a very powerful role in how the sport experience affects children both on and off the field.

CHAPTER EIGHT

Great Expectations

"Often they may just expect too much." *Male, 17, swimming*

How far do you expect your child to progress in sport? Do you think your child is good enough to pursue a career in professional sport or compete in the Olympics? Or do you think that your child's ability will limit him or her to pursuing sport at a purely recreational level? Have you ever considered questions such as these before? Should you?

These questions and their answers may not seem very important, but experience suggests otherwise. It has been known for a long time that expectations influence accomplishments. One of the first revelations of this came in Rosenthal and Jacobson's (1968) classic work on teacher expectations and student achievement in the classroom.

The Self-Fulfilling Prophecy

Rosenthal and Jacobson induced false expectations in a number of elementary school teachers by telling them that some of their students were intellectual "bloomers." The teachers were informed that these students could be expected to demonstrate large gains in academic performance during the forthcoming year because they had demonstrated good ability on several independent tests. By the end of the school year, these students did record significantly greater gains on standard achievement tests than other students in the same classrooms.

The interesting twist in this is that there were no real differences (in terms of initial ability or potential for intellectual gains) between those identified as "bloomers" and those who were not. The experimenters had simply told the teachers that certain students would do well, without any supporting evidence. Apparently, the stated expectations became a self-fulfilling prophecy—the "bloomers" actually did improve more academically than the other children.

Why did this occur? It is believed that individuals form their expectations of others using cues, such as previous interactions, past records, intelligence, physical attributes, sex, and so on. They then transmit these expectations to the other individual, both verbally, through praise or criticism, etc., and nonverbally, through smiles, or frowns, etc.

It is generally found that teachers demand better results from, and give more praise to, children for whom they hold high expectations. At the same time, teachers tend to interact differently with children for whom they hold lesser expectations. They are more likely to accept poor performances from these children and when they do well, these students are less likely to receive praise.

The basic point is simple, but very important: Our behaviors and attitudes toward people change quite dramatically depending on whether we hold a high or low expectation of success for them. And, as the above evidence suggests, individuals we expect a lot from tend to be the recipients of behaviors that are more conducive to being successful. Now, what about situations outside of the classroom? Do expectations play any role in other settings?

Research has revealed that expectations also play a role in sports. For example, it has been found that basketball players from whom the coach expected more (i.e., those players whom the coach perceived as being highest in ability) received more reinforcement than those players who were perceived by the coach to be low in ability (Rejeski, Darracott & Hutslar, 1979).

The expectations of parents also influences the performance of young athletes. According to Bloom (1982), parents' belief that their child, at five to eight years of age, had special qualities made a large difference to their expectations for the child and their methods of dealing with the child. Bloom concluded that these beliefs and expectations played a central role in the early, as well as the later, attainment of high levels of sports ability.

Expectations not only influence what a child achieves on the sports field, but also play a role in the development of the child off the sports field. For instance, expectations can often influence a child's self-esteem.

It is generally accepted that parents who provide encouragement and positive feedback to their children raise the level of their children's self-esteem. Having said that, however, problems can often arise when a parent's expectations do not match those of the child.

Mismatching

It is an established fact that children tend to look for similarities between how they see themselves and how others see them. When their perception of themselves matches what they think others think of them, there is no problem. However, when there is a mismatch, there is a problem. The child must decide who is right. This is confusing to the child and often negatively effects the child's psychological development.

The sporting field is one of the critical areas in which differences in judgments about the child can emerge. These differences generally take one of two forms. On the one hand, parents may perceive the child's ability to be much higher than the child does. This situation is typically associated with B-parents. Such parents have expectations that are above what the children think they can accomplish. This creates problems because wanting parental approval is a normal part of growing up. When expectations are too high, the children start to feel like failures because they can never please their parents.

B-parents tend to grab the headlines in the popular press because of the problems they cause through unrealistically high expectations, but problems also surface when children see their own sports abilities as being considerably higher than what they perceive their parents' ratings of those abilities to be. This confuses the young athletes—they wonder why their parents are not supporting their involvement in sport. And this can be just as damaging to the child's psychological development as the parent who is "too" supportive. C-parents are often guilty of not acknowledging their child's successes as much as they could.

The results of a recent study involving approximately two thousand children participating in sport are very clear on this point. The results revealed that where differences existed between the children's perceptions of their abilities and of their parents', the children's level of self-esteem was low. However, when the perceptions of the parents and the child were similar, the child's level of self-esteem was significantly higher (McElroy & Kirkendall, 1981).

Evidence such as this suggests that it would pay dividends for you, as a parent, to find out how your children assess their ability, and how they think you assess it. And while we are on the topic of assessing ability, just how well do parents know their child's actual abilities?

Assessing Ability

Although there is no current evidence available on the assessment of a child's sporting abilities by parents, there is evidence from other settings. In one very revealing study, parents were asked to estimate the performance of their grade one children on a series of intellectual and developmental tests (Miller, 1986).

The results indicated that parents were only moderately accurate in estimating their child's performance. Of special interest was the fact that whenever errors in judgment were made, parents tended to overestimate their child's abilities. While similar errors in assessment have not yet been documented in the sports setting, my interactions with parents over the years suggests a similar pattern.

One other noteworthy finding emerged from this study. It was found that the more accurate the parent was in estimating the child's performance, the better the child's performance. Is this coincidence, or is there something more tangible here? Probably the latter. After all, when parents know their child's abilities, they will be in a better position to create a learning environment that is appropriate, yet challenging, for the child. The sport environment is likely to be no different.

The question now is: How can you maximize the positive effects of expectations while minimizing their negative effects? Here are some suggestions that A-parents follow:

Accuracy

As noted previously, the more accurate our perceptions of a child's ability are, the more effective our expectations for the child will be. How accurate can we expect our perceptions of our child's sporting ability to be? If we do not have any formal training in the sport in which the child is participating, then it will be difficult for us to be objective and accurate in our assessments. Even trained personnel have difficulty in being objective because, quite often, "we see what we want to see."

Indeed, one study revealed that the expectations and performance ratings that trained gymnastic judges had of gymnasts were heavily influenced by the gymnasts' order of performance. In this study, the judges were asked to score taped gymnastic routines. Judges in one group were shown routines by gymnasts as they would appear in their natural order, whereas judges in another group were shown the identical performances, but in the reverse order of presentation. (For those of you who are not familiar with gymnastics, team order is standardized; weaker competitors perform before the stronger ones. Therefore, a gymnast performing a routine near the end of the team order would be expected to be better and, as a result, score higher.)

The results of this study revealed just that—judges awarded higher scores to those gymnasts performing near the end of the order, regardless of their actual performance (Ansorge, Sheer, Laub & Howard, 1978). What the judges expected to observe, they observed. The same thing can happen to parents. So, what's to be done?

The best way to get an accurate assessment of your child's ability is to ask for the opinion of your child's coach. If you think that your child has the ability to pursue a career in sport, it might be wise to secure a second opinion from another coach—one who has experience in identifying the characteristics of potential champions.

Matching

While accuracy is important in assessing your child's level of ability, it is of equal importance that your assessment of your child's ability and your child's assessment are consistent. As mentioned previously, judgments that are not compatible can result in problems, in both the child's on- and off-field development.

Remember, even if you and the coach "know" that your child is highly skilled and destined for a successful career, problems will arise if your child sees it differently. It is the child who must perform, not you.

How often do these differences occur? We're not sure, but we do know that differences do exist between how children and parents view what the other is doing. For example, in one ice-hockey study, parents reported that they did not give their sons instructions during the games, whereas a number of their sons felt that they did. Furthermore, most of the parents reported that their actions and comments toward the referees, coaches, and opposing players were generally positive, whereas their sons were not so sure (McClements, Fry & Sefton, 1982). The point of this example is that we can't always be sure that we are conveying the messages that we think we are. You must find out what your child thinks.

One of the best ways to obtain this information is to ask your children how good they think they are in their chosen sport. Do they think that they are better than most kids, about the same as most kids, or not as good as most kids? When you have their response to this question, ask them what they think your response as a parent would be to the same question. Do your parents think that you are better than most kids, about the same as most kids, or not as good as most kids?

The responses to these two questions will allow you to see whether there is a discrepancy between what your children see as their ability level and what they think you see. This information can then be used to choose an appropriate course of action.

For instance, if your children think that you rate their ability higher than they rate it, it would be wise for you to lower your expectations, at least for the time being. On the other hand, if your children rate their ability higher than you do, it would be appropriate to offer them more support and encouragement.

Flexibility

Parents must also be prepared to be flexible in their expectations for their children. As children pass through different stages of development, parents should modify their expectations.

For instance, as noted previously, children who undergo rapid growth spurts may suddenly develop problems in performing skills which previously they performed well. Since the children now have a body with a new shape, a number of old skills will have to be relearned. Maintaining the same expectations for the child that were held before the growth spurt is not the answer. Rather, the parent should reassure the child and, at the same time, lower their performance expectations until the child's physiological changes settle down.

There is another good reason for lowering our expectations under such conditions. In sports that require long-term bouts of intensive training, such as swimming, gymnastics, and ballet, children become more susceptible to injuries during periods of rapid growth. Consequently, during these periods, parents should lower their expectations in terms of the child's training load. The training load should be reduced until the growth spurt has abated. Only then should the normal training load be resumed.

One Size Does Not Fit All

Being fair to your children does not mean treating them all equally. Since your children are likely to differ developmentally, as well as in their skills and abilities, it is quite appropriate, and often desirable, that you hold different expectations for each of the children within your family.

A child who has been identified as having a high skill level would benefit much more from a parent's high demands for performance than would a child of lesser ability. In fact, the child of low ability is likely to become very frustrated by high demands, whereas the more highly skilled athlete is likely to be motivated by them. Remember, not everyone is going to be like Wayne Gretsky.

Furthermore, the children who feel that they cannot match their parents' expectations usually very quickly lose motivation. And because they are less motivated, they often perform at a lower level that is consistent with their belief in their ability, thus perpetuating the idea that they are less skilled and cannot improve! In other words, holding high expectations for children of lesser skill will not serve to raise their performance, but will rather work against them. Therefore, it would be a mistake to hold similar expectations for children who differ in ability. The expectation must fit the child's ability level.

Striving to Win

There is, however, one expectation that parents can feel confident in having for all children—the expectation that the children will always put forth the optimal effort in pursuit of their individual goals. Whether the children's current skill level is high or low, the expectation that children will strive for their goals is a good one.

Parents can best convey this idea to a child by rewarding the child's effort as much as the outcome. For instance, the parent should reward not only the young baseball player who runs hard to beat out an infield hit, but also the player who runs hard but is thrown out. It has been my experience that parents are more likely to praise the first individual than the second. That is unfortunate, because both players have tried hard. In fact, it is the second player who probably needs the praise more because the objective of the game, getting to first base safely, was not achieved. Parents who reward effort will never have to fear that a losing outcome will reduce a child's motivation.

What have you learned in this chapter that will allow you to become more like an A-parent? The key points to remember are as follows. Expectations are very powerful determinants of behavior. It would pay dividends if your expectations about your child's skills, abilities, and aspirations matched those of your child. If you do not know if your expectations match those of your child, it would be wise to find out. You can use the exercises in this chapter to get started.

We started this chapter by asking if you thought your child was good enough to pursue a career in elite sport. The "nuts and bolts" of aspiring toward a career in elite sports will be pursued in the next chapter.

CHAPTER NINE

Move Over, Mary Lou

"My goal, which I've always had, was to win a gold medal at the Olympics." *Anne Ottenbrite, 1984 L.A. gold medalist, swimming*

As in all endeavors in life, there is a pinnacle in sports. Whether it be at the national, international, or professional level, it represents the best that sports have to offer.

For those who reach this pinnacle, the rewards can be great. The sizable monetary rewards of many professional sports are widely publicized, and can amount to millions of dollars over the course of a career.

Dollars and Sense

As an example, let's look at the packages offered to two recent entrants into the ranks of professional sports.

Vinny Testaverde was the twenty-three-year-old who won the Heisman Trophy as America's best college football player. He was also the number one pick in the 1987 National Football League draft of college players. As a reward for his efforts, he reportedly signed an $8.2 million, six-year contract with the professional football team, Tampa Bay.

While this package was substantial, basketball player David Robinson received an even more impressive offer. Robinson, the top pick in the 1987 National Basketball Association draft of college players, reportedly signed a contract with the professional team, the San Antonio Spurs, worth between $24 and $30 million over the next eight years. What makes this offer even more remarkable is the fact that Robinson indicated that he still wanted to fulfil his two-year service commitment to the Navy before starting his professional career.

There are few non-sporting professions that would offer "entry-level" salaries of this magnitude. Although these examples are of unique individuals with exceptional talent, the "average" professional athlete is also adequately rewarded.

In American professional football, for instance, the average player's annual salary and benefits in 1987 exceeded $250,000. Major league baseball players average pay in 1987, including incentives, was $402,094. In that same season, fifty-eight players were reported to have made more than $1 million in salaries, including six who pulled in more than $2 million.

Elite athletes participating in so-called "amateur" events, such as the Olympics, also fare very well monetarily. Their reward does not come in the form of a salary, but they do very well with prize money and personal appearance fees.

Consider the case of Canadian sprinter Ben Johnson. After breaking the world record in the 100 meter sprint, Johnson can now command an appearance fee of up to $40,000 to compete indoors in 50-60 meter sprints at U.S. track meets. This fee is part of a package that also requires promotional activities, such as participating in media conferences. It is estimated that Johnson's earnings could reach $1 million if he wins a gold medal at the next Olympics.

Johnson is not the only person who has fared well because of his success in "amateur" sports. It has been reported that star hurdler Edwin Moses commands fees of up to $25,000 to compete in high-profile track meets. Rob de Castella, the Australian marathon great, reportedly received $150,000 for simply showing up and performing a number of public relation functions at the 1987 Boston Marathon. De Castella collected an additional $8,500 for finishing sixth in the marathon and the prize money for the winners of the race was more substantial. The winners of the men's and women's section of the 1987 marathon each received prize money of $40,000 plus a new Mercedes Benz—not a bad reward for less than three hours of work.

Other examples exist, but it should now be patently clear that a career in sports can make good economic sense. Furthermore, salaries and prize money are quite often only the tip of the iceberg. The "perks" of the sporting profession exceed those of other professions.

For instance, success in sports often translates into opportunities to endorse commercial products. NHL superstar Wayne Gretzky, in addition to earning a generous annual income from hockey, receives substantial sums of money from his endorsements of a number of products. And, in case you hadn't noticed, the majority of Miller Lite beer commercials feature former athletes.

A successful sports career can also lead to book publication. Chicago Bears quarterback Jim McMahon and his co-writer Bob Verdi reportedly received a six-figure advance from their publisher for the book *McMahon!* It has been projected that the total hardcover and paperback royalties due to McMahon may reach $1 million. Pete Rose, the baseball legend, and his co-writer reportedly received a $1-million advance on Rose's soon-to-be-released book.

Many athletes have converted great sporting careers into successful post-sports careers in acting, politics, and broadcasting. Broadcasting can be especially promising. For while there are undoubtedly a number of prerequisites to becoming a broadcaster, one of the best is a successful sporting career. Consider the case of veteran CBS sportscaster Pat Summerall. Summerall parlayed a successful career in professional football into a career as a sportscaster that rewards him annually with over $1 million.

A successful career in sports also often brings fame along with it. Mary Lou Retton, the American gymnast, is a recent example of an "amateur" athlete who turned an Olympic gold medal into fame and fortune. Following her gold-medal performance at the 1984 Olympics, Mary Lou's picture was featured on the cover of *Time*, *Newsweek*, and *Sports Illustrated*—all in the same week! She was also featured on the Wheaties's cereal box and was *Seventeen* magazine's cover girl. Because of her success, she performed with Bob Hope in his Christmas special, was a presenter at the annual Emmy Awards ceremonies, appeared in the Macy's Thanksgiving Day parade, and sat in a box seat at the World Series. She was also mentioned in a "Doonesbury" cartoon, where she was listed as an American heirloom alongside Old Glory and nuclear superiority!

The fruits of Mary Lou's labors represent an impressive list of rewards and honors, as measured by anyone's standards. Yet, while her "booty" sounds impressive, you may wish to think about the following before you rush out to enroll your child in an elite sports program.

The Numbers Game

Before you decide that a life in sport wouldn't be such a bad thing for your children, let's put the Mary Lou Rettons of the world into perspective. For every Mary Lou in the world, there are literally thousands of other aspiring athletes who tried to make it, but who did not. The odds against success are staggering.

What, for example, are the chances that your son will ever play in the Superbowl, the championship sporting event that most Americans would most like to attend? In any given year, there are about one million boys playing high school football in the U.S., but fewer than thirty thousand college players, of whom only a handful ultimately sign professional contracts. As you can see, the chances of making it to the Superbowl are slim at best. The attrition rates are similar for most sports.

Even those who become professional athletes aren't guaranteed a long and prosperous career. Football players, on average, can expect a career to last about 3.5 years, basketball players can expect 3.8 years, and baseball players can revel in the thought that their career will, on average, last 4.9 years. These figures suggest that anyone looking for long-term prospects may want to think twice before selecting a career in sports.

The Costs of Not Making It

What are the costs associated with not making it? Is it as simple as nothing ventured, nothing gained? Not really. Often individuals who do not make it not only lose out on the acclaim and monetary rewards associated with an Olympic medal or a professional contract, they also lose a large portion of their youth to the rigorous time schedules required when training for an elite event.

Although it is difficult to measure this last factor, the losses in terms of a normal social development alone can be considerable. Young female gymnasts, for instance, may train up to thirty hours each week. Swimmer Alex Baumann, the dual gold medalist at the 1984 Olympics, was training five hours per day for 340 days each year at the height of his career.

As you might imagine, it is very difficult to have a "normal" childhood under these conditions. In fact, in a recent newspaper interview, Baumann admitted that he would tell his own kids to pick a different sport. One aspiring young runner also made this point very clearly when he confided to me, "I want to stop running competitively so that I can be like my friends again."

Family Commitment

In addition to the costs that the children must pay for their climb to the top, a cost must also be extracted from their parents. Parents cannot afford the luxury of sitting on the sidelines as their children advance to the top of the sporting ladder. They must be actively involved at all levels.

This was made very clear in some recent work examining elite athletes and their coaches conducted by educator Benjamin Bloom and his colleagues (Bloom, 1982). In his three-year project, Bloom wanted to identify the special characteristics of individuals who had attained world-class status in a number of areas of achievement, including swimming and tennis. He was also interested in determining how important coaches and parents were in the athlete's climb to the top.

One of Bloom's most striking findings was the very active role that the family played in supporting and encouraging aspiring athletes at each stage of their development. Bloom suggested that not one of the elite swimmers or tennis players that he studied would have succeeded alone.

You should also be aware that your commitment to your child's rise through the ranks of sport requires more than mere support and encouragement. There are other costs involved, such as money, time, and general family disruption.

Money

Getting to the top costs money! Besides the costs of buying all the latest clothing and equipment, money may have to be spent on paying coaches. Elite, or would-be elite, athletes need full-time coaches, and full-time coaches need to make a living.

Further because the best coaches are few and far between, relocation may be necessary. Mary Lou Retton, for instance, moved from her home in West Virginia to Texas to train with her elite coach, Bela Karolyi. In such cases, room and board can form part of the cost of becoming one of the elite.

Other costs could be mentioned, but I think the point is clear—getting to the top is not without its monetary penalties. Before you get too discouraged, however, think about the cost of getting ahead in other fields. For instance, at current rates, it would cost your children $13,300 per year to attend the Harvard Business School. Getting ahead in most fields has its price!

Time

As progress is made in the sport, the family needs to devote more of its time to the child. This can result in other siblings being "short-changed": the "elite" child becomes the center of attention and, as a result, commands a disproportionate amount of the family's time. It is not that these increased demands for time are the result of selfishness on the part of the child; they are, rather, the result of the increasing demands being placed on the child. Nevertheless, the result is the same—more time being spent on the "elite" child.

Family Disruption

Special arrangements for meals, travel, and other incidentals become increasingly necessary as the child advances. That may mean that the rest of the family has to make sacrifices. Any resemblance to the typical stereotype of a happy family will likely be more by accident than by design.

The costs associated with being the parents of an elite athlete are summed up by Mary Lou Retton in the dedication to her recent book, *Mary Lou*: "To my parents, who have sacrificed a part of their lives for me."

What's It Going To Be?

The point of the preceding discussion has not been to scare you into eliminating a sports career from your children's goals, but rather to make you aware of the fact that the climb to the top of the sporting ladder is not without its demands. The days of someone making it to the top through sheer talent and energy are long gone if, indeed, they ever existed. Furthermore, the trip to the top does not happen fortuitously. It needs to be planned, and planning starts with a decision. So, what's it going to be, a shot at the big time, or involvement at a purely recreational level?

Since the decision to go for the "big one" entails a much different and more onerous path, it should be made with some care. Although it is not the right decision for everyone, there will always be people interested in it. For this reason, I have included a section on what information parents should look for if they feel they have another Mary Lou or Wayne Gretzky on their hands.

Gifted Children

Is it possible to identify qualities in your children that will mark them as "gifted" and destined for success? As you might guess, the answer is probably *no*. Bloom in his research on talent development, was also interested in knowing whether current elite athletes were so rare and unusual as children that their special human qualities or "gifts" could be identified even at an early age.

Bloom's (1982) investigation revealed that champion performers may have been favored by small differences in relevant physical and psychological characteristics. However, their ultimate success was largely dependent on the support and coaching they received over a long period of time, more than a decade in most instances. While heredity certainly establishes the upper bounds of the athlete's ability, other factors are crucial in determining how close one comes to that potential. Most top performers are not "natural-born" athletes, but rather highly trained individuals who have reached the top by developing their talents through hard work and dedication within a very strong support system.

Bloom also identified three important factors that characterized the elite athletes when they were younger. Let's see if your children have "star" potential.

The Big Three

Willingness To Work

Those individuals who eventually became champions exhibited a strong willingness to work hard at improving themselves in their sport. It is worth noting, however, that this characteristic was not highly evident in these people from five to eight years of age, but only later, after several years of instruction. All of you

B-parents should note that this willingness to work was generally child-initiated, not the result of adult influences.

Competitiveness

Individuals who became champions also exhibited a very keen competitive spirit when they were young. But so do most children. When we ask children why they participate in organized sport, the thrill of competition usually ranks in the top five reasons. However, in the children who eventually make it to the top, this competitive spirit tends to be more pronounced. These children train solely to excel.

Learning Rates

The final quality noted in these children was the ability to learn new skills and techniques rapidly. For instance, a number of the Olympic swimmers that Bloom studied had often won local swimming contests after very little instruction, even when their competitors may have had very good instruction for longer periods of time.

This penchant for rapid learning was usually restricted to the sport being played. The swimmers, for instance, would not have been able to exhibit the same rapid learning rate on the tennis court. In other words, these budding stars were not "natural-born" athletes in any sport they tried.

With a Little Help From Their Friends

Although rapid learning can be attributed to some extent to specialized body functions, such as good hand-eye coordination, good dexterity, or good balance, these attributes would not have been advantageous to the developing athlete if they had not been further enhanced by instruction and encouragement from parents and coaches.

The Effect of Parental Interests

Although children may have specific qualities that make them particularly suitable for some activities and not for others, Bloom believes that the values and interests of the parents will determine which activities are pursued.

"I don't like hockey but dad played and he likes me to play."
Male, 11, hockey

In a home where interest in sport predominates, a child's interest in, or ability to play, the flute will probably not be noted as being important. Consequently, the child is not likely to receive any significant instruction or encouragement in music, and a very promising career may never get off the ground. Children generally receive encouragement and coaching in some talent area first, and then later parents and/or coaches identify some unusual talent that should be pursued further. However, this process is often short-circuited if the interests of the parents are elsewhere.

Parents mustn't forget that their interests and encouragement may well influence what their children eventually pursue. It pays, therefore, to keep an open mind in terms of your child's interests and aptitudes. Not every child is destined to become a superstar in sport. It would be a pity if children missed an opportunity to pursue an activity suited to their interests or skills just because a parent had different interests.

Master Coaches

As noted previously, coaches play a very important role in getting young athletes to the top. The athlete's final coach is very critical in this regard. These final coaches, or master coaches, generally have the time to deal with only a few athletes at any one time and because there are only a handful of these master coaches scattered throughout the country, they can be quite selective in choosing the athletes they will coach. Let's take a look at what criteria they use to select prospective athletes (Bloom,1982).

Advanced Standing

As you might expect, one of the things that master coaches look for is a level of competence far above the average. In swimming, for example, the prospective swimmers will have already completed successfully at their age levels, as judged by standards such as local and national age-group records.

Self-discipline

The master coach will also look for young athletes who already possess the discipline and the desire to work hard for extended periods of time. Ability and skill are not enough. According to master coaches, undisciplined athletes or those who are unwilling to accept a rigorous training schedule, are to be avoided at all costs. The master coach does not want to be a motivator, but rather a teacher.

The young athletes who have this discipline develop it because the desire to become a great athlete means more to them than anything else in the world. How do you know if your child has this discipline? Although there are no sure-fire methods to determine this, young athletes who are already putting more time into their sport than into any other part of their lives will probably be disciplined enough to handle the tough training regimen associated with becoming a world-class athlete.

Desire to Excel

Budding champions must possess a strong desire to excel. They must believe that, with the proper training and preparation, they will become one of the greats in their sport. They need to know very early in their sporting careers that they want to be the best. Canadian swimmer Anne Ottenbrite is typical in this regard. When Anne started swimming at thirteen years of age, she determined that she would one day win a gold medal at the Olympics. As a result, she worked very long and hard, and in the 1984 Olympics, she achieved her goal by winning the gold medal in the 200-meter breaststroke.

Fast Learners

Master coaches also look for young athletes who can learn quickly. They want an athlete who can overcome a particular problem with a minimum of instruction and explanation. For instance, an aspiring tennis player who is told to make some adjustment to his serve should be able to do so quickly, with a minimum of error.

These are the characteristics that your children will need if they are to have any chance of achieving world-class status in the sporting arena. Now that you know what these characteristics are, and the odds against becoming a champion, you should be in a much better position to make an objective assessment of your children's chances of making it to the top.

Finally, if your children decide that this is what they want to do, and it should be stressed that it is *their* decision, you should be like A-parents and always remember that your role will be critical in determining whether or not your children reach that ultimate objective.

In our discussion on identifying potential elite athletes, we briefly mentioned the importance of coaches. The next chapter extends this discussion by looking at the types of coaches that may be best suited for your child.

CHAPTER TEN

Selecting a Coach

"He's taking me from nowhere to somewhere." *Male, 14, swimming*

Kicking the Tires

Selecting a coach for your child is *not* like buying a used car! Absolutely correct, you say. After all, your child is much more valuable than a car. You can't put a price on your child, whereas a car certainly has a price. You can't replace your child, whereas a car is a temporary investment that will, some day, be replaced. Your child will improve with age, whereas the car will deteriorate.

If you're thinking that it is ridiculous to compare the value of your children to the value of a used car, you're right. However, I used the analogy for two reasons. First, I hoped that it would draw your attention to the importance of a coach in your child's sporting life. Second, many parents spend more time buying a used car, even if it's only the time taken to "kick the tires," than they do when selecting a coach for their child.

Importance of the Coach

Although parents are patently important in their children's sporting lives, it is without doubt the coaches who exert the greatest influence on the young athletes—a fact the athletes themselves recognize. For instance, world-class female swimmers reported in one study that their former coaches were still the most significant adults in their lives six to twelve years after they had finished competing.

Bearing this in mind, one wonders why so many parents trust their child's welfare to a coach about whom they know little or nothing. Worse than that, many parents admit to having doubts about youth sport coaches. The *Miller Lite Report*, for instance, revealed that 82 percent of all parents questioned thought that amateur team coaches often take the game too seriously. Yet, every season, children are entrusted to "unknown" coaches. Why?

- Maybe it was convenient.
- Maybe the parents didn't know any better.
- Maybe they hadn't thought of it before.
- Maybe they didn't have enough time to check the coach out.

Although these are all plausible explanations, they are not, from my perspective, good enough. Parents *should* take the time to find out about the coach that their child will be associated with over the course of the season. You wouldn't, or at least you shouldn't, send your child to a doctor or a dentist you hadn't already checked out so why should it be any different when selecting a coach? The effects that a coach can have on your child can be powerful and long-lasting. At the very least, why miss out on an opportunity to enhance your child's growing years by not looking for an appropriate coach?

Coaching Qualities

What should you look for in a coach? First of all, there is no such thing as an ideal coach. But, then, it would be hard to find an ideal member of any profession, be it medicine, law, education, business or the arts. However, as in most professions, there are certain qualities characteristic of the better practitioners.

The rest of this chapter outlines the qualities that you should look for when evaluating your child's coach. However, keep in mind that you are unlikely to find any coach , anywhere, who meets all of the criteria listed. Your goal should be to find a coach who exhibits most of these characteristics and is compatible with your child.

Compatibility

What do we mean by compatibility? Like most things in life, the best outcomes are the results of the right mix of ingredients. Furthermore, what's right for one individual may not be right for another. It's somewhat like drinking scotch whiskey. Some people find scotch mixes well with water, while others prefer soda, and still others prefer coke.

The best outcomes in sport will occur when your child "mixes" well with the coach. There are no hard and fast rules on how to get the correct mix; however, there are some things that you should consider. One of the main considerations should be your child's personality. For instance, shy, introverted children should not be placed in the care of a loud, demonstrative coach. The interaction with a coach such as this will do nothing to enhance the child's enjoyment of the sport and may, in fact, contribute to the child's withdrawal from it.

You should also gauge how your child reacts to failure. If your child shies away from public criticism, a demanding coach who reacts to your child's mistakes publicly and blatantly is not likely to be the best coach for your child.

Finally, you should also try to assess how quickly your child picks up new sports skills. If your child generally has trouble picking up new skills, it would be wise to seek out a coach who demonstrates patience and who allows your child to progress at a slower rate without making the child feel inadequate—a big order to fill by anyone's standards, but not impossible.

Now that we've looked at compatibility let's examine the general qualities that "good" coaches exhibit. Bear in mind that, in this book, "good" describes a coach who creates an environment where your child will grow both as an athlete and as a human being.

Different Strokes

Your children will probably be exposed to different coaches as they progress through the ranks of sport; how many depends on a number of factors, such as the number of sports played by your child, the number of times you relocate, and how far your child progresses. World-class athletes are often exposed to three or four different coaches in their climb to the top.

Bloom's findings in his study of elite athletes and their coaches are very revealing in terms of the coach's influence on the athlete. Bloom (1982) found, for instance, that Olympic swimmers typically had about three coaches during their years of training, which generally lasted about ten years. These coaches differed in some very important ways, with the first coach being significantly different from the final coach. Let's look at the qualities of the "good" first coach and the "good" final coach, as revealed by Bloom.

The First Exposure

A child's first experience with a coach is often the most important in the individual's entire sporting career. Since sport is (or should be) a voluntary affair, the first experience may determine whether the child stays with sport or drops out altogether. Children who enjoy sport continue in it; those who don't tend to drop out. What are the characteristics of first coaches that are remembered by athletes who enjoyed their sporting experiences so much that they carried on to become world-class athletes?

Characteristics

• Friendly First coaches are often remembered by elite athletes as being friendly.

• Encouraging They are also remembered for the great encouragement they provided to the young athletes when they were first being introduced to the sport.

• Motivating Champion athletes remembered that their first coaches were individuals who initially motivated them to explore the sport in a playful way. In other words, they tended to make the experience fun and enjoyable.

A closer look at these qualities reveals a common thread. First coaches tended to be child-oriented rather than sport-oriented. In fact, if one quality stood out amongst them, it was their effectiveness in dealing with young children. These first coaches were remembered fondly by these outstanding athletes many years later, not for their technical expertise or sporting prowess, but for their *personal* qualities!

It appears, then, that the most important quality to look for in your child's first coach is the "personal" factor. There will be plenty of time for your child to learn skills as the years progress, but there will be only one initiation into organized sport. For the sake of the child, let's hope that it is an enjoyable and rewarding one.

Good first coaches display certain types of on-field behavior. Obviously, coaches must know what they are doing and take adequate safety precautions, but there are other qualities to look for that can provide clues as to how the experience of working with a coach will turn out for your child. A "good" first coach is likely to:

• Give more encouragement and compliments than criticism.

• Critisize the behavior to be corrected rather than the child (e.g., "Your toss was too low" rather than "That was a stupid serve").

• Be patient when the children are learning the skills.

• Encourage the children to feel good about themselves, regardless of the outcome.

• Reward the children's attempts as much as the outcome.

• Make practice as much fun as playing.

• Recognize and encourage the contribution of all players.

• Help the children understand that as long as they try, they can never be losers.

In a nutshell, the best first coach is the one who will put your child first, and the game second.

The Master Coaches

On the other end of the coaching continuum is the master coach. The master coach is the one who will take your child to the pinnacle of performance. Obviously, not everyone will reach this level, nor should everyone want to. But there needs to be some pinnacle of excellence toward which, those who wish to, may strive.

If so few children are going to get to the pinnacle, why even mention master coaches? Two reasons. For one, some parents will have children who have reached a stage where a master coach is required. The characteristics outlined below should provide them with some information that will assist them in identifying that special coach.

Another reason for outlining the qualities of a master coach is to show that a master coach would not be appropriate as your child's first coach. Quite simply, master coaches are too demanding and generally do not have the time or patience to allow young athletes the time to develop the skills necessary for success in sport. Seeking a master coach as your child's first coach may sound good in theory, but it is likely to result in a sporting experience that is less than positive for all concerned. It would be like starting your child's piano lessons by engaging a concert pianist!

Before we proceed, a warning about planning. If your child is in need of a master coach, you should be aware that selecting one is often a very time-consuming process requiring a large amount of care and planning. The selection of a master coach for some sports may take as much as one to two years. As a result, you should be very certain that your child wants to pursue a sports career and possesses both the technical skills and psychological make-up to be considered as a candidate for a master coach. The information in the preceding chapter should help you make this decision more objectively.

Now, let's have a closer look at the qualities of a master coach, as identified by Bloom and his colleagues. Some of the most important qualities are as follows:

Authoritarian

The master coach speaks, and expects to be obeyed. Criticisms, explanations, or standards set by the master coach demand action. They are not open to question or debate.

This is not a new finding—previous research has illustrated that as athletes mature, they tend to prefer a more authoritative coaching style (Chelladurai & Carron, 1979). They want to be told what to do and when. However, this is not the case with younger athletes. They tend to prefer a more democratic style of coaching. They are still learning and discovering, and they appreciate freedom to explore. This is one of the reasons why a master coach would not serve the purposes of a first-time athlete very well.

High Expectations

One of the greatest qualities of master coaches is their ability to instil in young athletes the expectation that they can and will become great athletes. This expectation is conveyed in a number of different ways. Some of the more common ones include:
- Special treatment of the athlete.
- Giving attention to the athletes in the presence of others.
- What is said to the athlete.

• What is said to others about the athlete.

All of these combine to communicate to the athletes that they are very special and fully capable of being the best around.

Motivator

As you might expect, master coaches are great motivators. But the way they motivate may surprise you. They do not motivate through praise, but rather through emphasis on progress and improvement.

Motivation is simple. Goals are set by the master coach and the athlete's motivation comes through continually attempting to achieve these goals and then moving on to greater ones. When a goal is accomplished, such as winning a major championship, the master coach is not likely to praise the athlete, but rather to identify errors that need to be corrected before the next major event. As mentioned elsewhere, this approach would be counterproductive for a young athlete who is still learning the game, as mistakes would be much more prevalent than positive performances.

Although the elite athlete is not generally praised for accomplishing goals, the individual is continually kept informed of the progress being made. In other words, the master coach is much more task-oriented than person-oriented, which is the exact opposite approach to that taken by the good first coach.

Public performances are also used extensively by master coaches as motivational techniques. Athletes are continually being entered into competitions where their skills can be tested against the best available talent. These comparisons provide information on how the athlete is progressing.

Once again, this is unlikely to be the best approach to take with children who are still learning the skills of a sport. For these children, the constant comparison of their skills to others' will only demonstrate their weaknesses. Children at this stage of development need to be exposed to the more positive aspects of sport, not to be reminded of their inadequacies.

But, what about the negative feedback that elite athletes receive when they are not successful in public events? Master coaches do not worry about the fact that these public contests may result in failure for the athletes. Rather, they use these failures as motivational tools.

They do this by identifying and pointing out to the athlete some of the positive aspects of the performance. These positive aspects are used as evidence that progress was made, even though the ultimate goal may not have been achieved. Furthermore, the master coach points out changes that will improve the performance in the future.

We can all learn something from how master coaches deal with failure. This is covered in more detail in the chapter "Handling Defeat."

Personal Relationships

The master coach, generally speaking, is not the "buddy" type. Very few befriend their charges. Most remain distant. Successful athletes often remember their former master coaches with gratitude, but rarely with warmth or affection.

Once again, this points out one of the the very important distinctions between first and master coaches. First coaches are more person-oriented, and are often remembered by their former athletes with affection, whereas master coaches are very much task-oriented. Keep this in mind when you are evaluating coaches for the different stages of your child's development.

It is hoped that the information in this chapter has provided you with some insights into what makes a good coach—first or master. It is also hoped that you will now be able to use this information to give your child the best possible sporting experience by matching up your child with an appropriate coach.

The next chapter addresses an issue that is close to the hearts of most coaches—the issue of parental behavior at games. We generally hear about the "game" behavior of parents through the media, here we will hear the story from the perspective of their children.

CHAPTER ELEVEN

Take Me Out to the Ball Game

"I like it most when my parents stay in the car." *Male, 14, baseball*

If you read the media reports, one thing is certain in children's sport—game days bring out the worst in parents! We're all aware of the bad publicity that some parents generate for themselves when they attend their children's sporting events—the stories of parents biting off the umpire's ear, yelling obscenities at players on both teams, fighting among themselves in the stands, or assuming the role of the coach by shouting instructions to their children from the sidelines.

It's true these behaviors do occur at games. In fact, the public acknowledgement of these occurrences has prompted certain critics of youth sport to suggest banning all parents from their children's games. That's right, it has been suggested that parents take their children to the ball game, but leave before it starts.

This might eliminate some of the problems cited above, but it would create other problems: children would lose their parents' support and encouragement during the contest, and parents would lose the opportunity to share in their children's on-field sporting accomplishments. It would also necessitate banning a very large number of parents. The *Miller Lite Report* revealed that 81 percent of parents frequently watch their children compete. That adds up to a lot of spectating parents!

So, what's the solution? The best answer comes from the children themselves. For a number of years, I have been collecting information concerning children's attitudes toward their parents' involvement in their sporting lives. What follows is a synopsis of how children view their parents' involvement on game days.

Are Parents Wanted?

Do children want their parents to be removed completely from the playing fields? No. For the most part, children *do* want their parents to attend their games and matches.

There are two reasons for this. First, as the following quotes indicate, children like to receive encouragement for their participation in sport.

"Mom and dad, mostly mom, attend all the sports matches I am involved in. I like having them there—they are a great support when my teams are doing badly; they cheer and they really get involved." *Female, 14, basketball*

"I like it when they come along and watch and see me do a good shot and say, 'Well done.'" *Male, 14, tennis*

"I like it when my mom and dad cheer me on when I'm playing." *Male, 12, basketball*

"I like it when they, or just one of them, come and watch me play." *Female, 14, softball*

"I like it when he encourages me and the teammates when I play football." *Male, 14, football*

Children need to feel supported in whatever they do, and your actual presence at their sporting events is one of the best ways to show this support.

A second reason for attending games is that parents who have viewed the contest will be in a much better position to discuss the event after it is over. Children generally enjoy this type of post-game interaction.

"My parents come to the matches. They seem to care about how I feel about the game I've just played." *Female, 12, tennis*

"I like it when they cheer me and ask me questions." *Female, 11, track*

Like most things in life, however, this post-game interaction should be done in moderation. Parents who inundate their children with questions about the event (B-parents are often guilty of this practice) often do more harm than good.

"I don't like it when they question me a lot." *Male, 11, swimming*

"They ask for too many details about it. A few is O.K., but they ask me lots." *Female, 13, softball*

"They spend ages explaining something to me that I did wrong." *Male, 12, basketball*

In addition to keeping this interaction short, it also pays to accentuate the positive aspects of the children's performance. Children, not surprisingly, are never too enthralled about being flooded with reminders of how badly they have performed. They know when they have not done well; they do not need to be reminded of it by others.

"I hate how they tell me all the bad things I do and not the good things." *Female, 12, basketball*

"I don't like them telling me after the game what I should have done." *Female, 14, softball*

"It annoys me when he tells me what I did wrong when I get off the tennis court." *Female, 13, tennis*

"I hate her telling me all the mistakes I've made when I come off the court." *Female, 16, tennis*

"I don't like it when my parents are disappointed in my performance, and so am I. They suggest reasons for improvement that I usually don't want to hear." *Male, 17, baseball*

This response to failure appears to be widespread. The *Miller Lite Report* revealed that 63 percent of parents react to children's losses in sport by suggesting how skills can be improved. While this might seem to be a good idea at the time, identifying your children's mistakes with a view to correcting them for future performances often backfires.

Why? For one thing, parents may not be great teachers because they have been around their children too much. Research on learning has revealed consistently that when an individual is either rewarded or punished too often, both rewards and punishments become less effective in learning new behavior. Since parents reward and punish their children each day, the influence of these reinforcements may be lost when parents attempt to teach their children sports skills. I am told by my friend Barry that his son tends to listen to and learn his baseball skills faster from his uncle than from him.

Other research also indicates that children are often motivated to work harder for strangers. This may be one of the reasons why children are more willing to put in extra practice time for the coach than they are for you.

Furthermore, children expect a coach to correct their mistakes. The coach is the expert. If mistakes are to be rectified, it is the job of the coach, not the parent. Unless the parents have a history as an athlete or coach in that sport, their words are likely to go unheeded. In fact, because they are not seen as experts, their attempts at correction often become a source of annoyance for the children.

"They put me down and criticize when they can do no better." *Male, 13, hockey*

"My dad puts me down because he thinks he knows everything about it, but he's never been involved in swimming." *Female, 15, swimming*

"I don't like my parents telling me what to do when I already know." *Male, 12, water polo*

"He makes me try his way when I think he's wrong." *Male, 13, tennis*

"Generally, my parents are good, except my dad tends to think he knows everything." *Female, 14, horse riding*

"My dad never played hockey and doesn't really understand how tired and frustrated the players can become when playing." *Male, 16, hockey*

If, however, your children perceive you to be an expert in their particular sport, then your attempts at helping your children to change their bad habits will be more readily received.

"When I play football, my dad can give me tips on what I'm doing wrong, because he played it too." *Male, 13, football*

Exceptions

Although children generally want parents to attend their games, there are some children who do not like their parents to watch them. Many of these children are reacting to their parents' poor behavior, but others simply get embarrassed when they are being watched. This often happens in the early stages of involvement in a sport, when children are still learning the skills, or in activities where it is easy to isolate the child's play. (For example, individual sports often make children more anxious than team sports because it is much easier to evaluate the child's performance.)

Although attendance by parents is important, parents must be aware that with certain children and in certain situations, attendance may not be for the best. To ensure that you are doing the right thing, you should ask your children if they want you to attend.

"I don't want them watching me play tennis, but I don't mind if they watch me play sports like softball." *Female, 14, tennis, softball*

"I hate it if mom comes. Sometimes, it's embarrassing in front of my friends. I wouldn't tell her though, I'd probably hurt her feelings." *Female, 11, tennis*

"When I compete in competitions, I do not like it when they come and watch." *Female, 12, gymnastics*

If however, your children do indicate that your attendance is important, the next question is: How often should parents attend the games?

Perfect Attendance?

Is it necessary that parents attend 100 percent of the games over the course of a season? This would show your children that you really care about their participation in sport, but, realistically, this is not practical or even necessary. The feeling that I get from a large number of children is that they are quite satisfied if their parents at least make an attempt to get to some of the games. However, it is worth remembering that unfulfilled promises for attendance are just as devastating to young children as the non-attendance of parents who are simply not interested.

"Dad says he'll come and doesn't." *Female, 12, basketball*

"I like them to come and watch, but often they can't." *Male, 14, rowing*

"They both have full time jobs but sometimes they take time off and come and see us play." *Female, 13, volleyball*

"Dad takes me and sometimes watches if he's not too busy." *Male, 16, baseball*

"They come along to as many games as they can." *Male, 16, football*

"Sometimes they can watch and they don't." *Female, 11, volleyball*

"I don't mind if they don't come and watch as long as they come occasionally and for the final." *Female, 14, basketball*

All right, now that you are convinced that your attendance, at least at some of your children's games, is important, the next issue concerns appropriate behavior.

How Should I Act?

Isn't making an appearance at your children's games enough? According to the children that I have talked to over the years, the answer is probably *no*. Children also want their parents to show some interest in what is happening to them on the field. Remember the last time you were at a party, and the person that you were talking to seemed more intent on looking over your shoulder than in listening to you? Not a very nice feeling, is it?

Parents who do not show any interest in what is happening on the field are running the risk of being D-parents. Children of D-parents tend to feel that they are not being supported in their sporting endeavors.

"I don't like it if they come and sit there as if they are bored." *Female, 12, gymnastics*

"I hate it when they sit like zombies, talk to other people, read." *Male, 14, soccer*

"They don't watch the game." *Male, 11, football*

"I don't like it when they eat chocolate when I'm playing." *Male, 11, soccer*

As you can see from the above comments, showing interest may be as simple as attentively watching the games your children are participating in. If you attend a game, make your presence known by taking a position in the stands where you can observe the game unhindered. Don't be like a friend of mine who confided to me that he often took up a position behind a tree whenever he watched his son play. Having been a professional athlete in the same sport, he was afraid that his own competitive background and his eye for picking out mistakes might make him too "pushy." As a result, his son lost an opportunity of seeing his father support his sporting career.

Furthermore, since this father, because of his former professional status, would likely have been perceived as an expert by his son, his son would most probably have received his father's comments in the proper vein—as helpful suggestions for improvement.

Besides watching attentively, there are also some things that parents should not do while watching the contest. These include the following:

Providing Instructions

Parents who yell instructions to their children while the game is in progress are likely doing more harm than good. For one thing, children may become distracted by such comments. Quite often, this distraction makes the children forget about what they are supposed to be doing and, as a result, their performance suffers.

"Dad sometimes tells me what to do when I'd rather play how I want to." *Male, 13, tennis*

"I hate the individual pressure. When he is behind the goal, he stands and tells me what to do." *Male, 12, soccer*

"I don't like it when they watch me because it puts me off and because they tell me what to do." *Male, 15, baseball*

"I don't like when she comes to me while I'm on the court and says things like, 'hit the ball harder than that.' " *Female, 11, tennis*

"It's awful when they try to tell me things while I'm still playing." *Female, 16, tennis*

"Yelling out things—'Come on, you can do it!'—Yuk, that makes me embarrassed." *Female, 14, volleyball*

By yelling instructions, you also put your children into the dilemma of deciding who to listen to—their parents or their coach. Children have enough to worry about during a game without this.

"I don't like it when he tries to tell me how to do it in different ways than the coach." *Male, 15, tennis*

Criticizing the Coach

I'm sure there will be times when you disagree with a coach's judgment. There may be times when you wonder why your children are not learning new skills, why they are not getting to play as much as the other children, or why they are being continually yelled at by the coach. You are certainly not out of order if you question your children's coach about these things. These are legitimate concerns. In fact, as a parent who is looking out for the welfare of your children, you would be remiss if you did not ask such questions. But they should be asked at the right time. To discuss issues such as these during practices or games and in front of your children will only create anxiety and confusion in your children. It would be much better to discuss issues that you deem important after the young athletes have departed.

Castigating Opposing Players, Their Parents and Officials

Although many adults consider it an inalienable right to heap abuse on the opposition, their parents, and even the officials, children see it differently. In fact, children often point out that they do not like or even condone such behavior.

"When they abuse the child that pushes me, I get embarrassed." *Female, 12, basketball*

"It embarrasses me when my parents swear at the referee." *Male, 15, hockey*

"I don't like it when they tell the umpire off." *Female, 14, swimming*

Aside from the effects on their own children, parents should also consider how their remarks affect other children. Young Brian Wiseman is a case in point.

Brian was an ice-hockey prodigy at ten years of age. He scored 413 goals in eighty games over the course of one season. You would have expected Brian to be admired for his accomplishments; instead, he was often the victim of the parents of opposing players who stood and yelled obscenities at him. Rather than feeling good about playing well, Brian recalled in an interview several years later that, "There were times...when I came home and I really didn't care if I played another game."

This seems like a terrible punishment for a ten-year-old boy whose only crime was that he was a good player. Spectating parents should keep in mind that they are not being entertained by competing adult professionals,they are watching children at play. Since Brian Wiseman was the victim of this mindless attention, it is only fitting that he have the last word, "It's not fair what they say. Let the kids play the game and have fun and if there's somebody playing better than your son, then that's the way it's meant to be."

Remember, too, that parents are also powerful models for children. How will our children ever learn such virtues as self-control and sportsmanship when their role models exhibit the opposite? As parents, it would pay to keep in mind the words of the French philosopher Joubert, "Children are in greater need of models than critics."

Being Overly Vocal

With the exception of D-parents, most parents like to get involved vocally at their children's games. This is verified by the *Miller Lite Report* which found that 83 percent of parents almost always or often shout encouragement when watching their children play. Encouragement is good for children, who for the most part, enjoy it. Unfortunately, that enjoyment is often dampened for a number of children by overzealous parents who draw attention to either themselves or their children by their ill-timed and vociferous remarks:

"They yell out and make fools of themselves." *Male, 14, rowing*

"I don't mind them coming to watch as long as they don't get too vocal." *Female, 14, softball*

"My parents are all right as long as they don't jump up and down screaming like idiots." *Female, 14, basketball*

"My parents are all right as long as they don't jump up and down screaming like idiots." *Female, 14, basketball*

"They can embarrass you when they tell you off in front of your friends." *Female, 14, tennis*

"I don't like it when they yell at me in the middle of the game and everybody stares at me." *Female, 14, basketball*

"I don't like them cheering me madly at the wrong times." *Female, 14, softball*

"It's embarrassing when they yell out when it's silent." *Female, 14, gymnastics*

So, for the sake of the children's enjoyment, act like A-parents, and think before you speak!

Children do enjoy the support and encouragement that they get from parents who attend their games, but they also expect certain behavior. As A-parents, you should be aware of your responsibilities when attending your children's games. After all, they are no more demanding than the rules of common courtesy.

This brings us to our final chapter. Perhaps, fittingly, it also deals with the final chapter in a child's sporting life—departure from sport.

CHAPTER TWELVE
Exiting Graciously

"Gymnastics is bad, but my parents like it." *Female, 11, gymnastics*

Although the thrust of this book has been on children's involvement in sport, there comes a time when children may want to leave sport. You may think, "What's the big deal with children wanting to leave sport?" Well, there are two things worth considering. First, if your children indicate a desire to leave sport, you should find out if they are leaving for the right reasons. Second, if they continue but don't seem to be having much fun, you should find out why they're staying! Let's consider each of these issues.

Reasons for Leaving Sport

There may come a time in your children's sporting life when they decide they want to "retire." It is probably in the best interests of your children to find out why this decision has been taken.

If the decision is based on the fact that the child's interest is simply in other activities, there is no reason for concern. Young athletes often tell us that they leave a particular sport because they have other things to do. Sport has no monopoly on children's enjoyment or character building. A myriad of other activities, in music, art, drama, and so forth, can also serve these functions and children should not be discouraged from pursuing them. Remember, sport is not for everyone.

If your children have sampled a number of sports, but are more interested in other, non-sporting activities, encourage them to pursue these other interests. If, however, your children indicate that their interests are elsewhere because of the negative experiences they have encountered in sport, then some self-analysis by parents may be in order.

Sometimes parents contribute to their children's premature departure from sport, without realizing what they are doing until it is too late. Early recognition of this tendency could help your children stay in sport longer and enjoy it more. Here are some reasons, relating to parents, that children give for dropping out of sports.

Not Liking the Pressure

Children often indicate that they leave sport because they do not like the pressure. Although this pressure can come from a number of sources, parents, especially B-parents, are often the primary source.

As indicated throughout this book, children often feel pressure when their parents consistently expect them to win. If this is the case, the parents should refocus from outcome to performance, based on the child's unique skills and abilities. Information in previous chapters has addressed this issue in some detail.

Not Receiving Enough Support

Some children who feel unduly pressured are often the victims of too much "support"; then there are others who indicate that they left sport because they did not get enough. Both D-parents and C-parents play a role in this, although their approaches are different.

As you will remember, D-parents are not really interested in the sporting accomplishments of their children. On the surface this may not seem important but, apparently, this so-called "neutrality" does not go unnoticed by some children. For instance, a recent study of young ice-hockey players and their parents found that the boys who dropped out of the hockey program had parents who attended less games and practices and, based upon their actions and comments, appeared less concerned or involved with their sons' hockey pursuits than the parents of players who continued playing. The message for D-parents is clear—get involved; support and encourage your child whenever possible.

C-parents can, in a slightly different way from D-parents, also contribute to children wanting to drop out of sport. C-parents are preoccupied with their children's enjoyment. So preoccupied, in fact, that the importance of winning is downplayed. But, as previously noted, winning is a valued goal in sport and should be acknowledged. Unfortunately, C-parents in their pursuit of enjoyment for their child, often fail to accord any significance to winning.

"Sometimes they cheer for the other team and that makes me mad." *Male, 12, soccer*

Apparently, some children pick up on this and see it as an important enough reason to get out of sport. The hockey study just mentioned, for instance, found that young ice-hockey players who quit the program received little acknowledgment for their good performances from their parents. When this expected acknowlegment was not forthcoming, some of these hockey players perceived this lack of support as sufficient reason to depart. So, a message to all you C-parents out there, winning is important. Don't be afraid to acknowledge it.

Too Time-Consuming

Sport takes time. But how much of a child's time should be devoted to any one sport? According to some children, not too much.

There is no magic formula to determine the optimal amount of time that should be spent on any one sport. Most of the problems with spending too much time stem from early specialization. The thinking behind early specialization is that to reach the top, young athletes must be identified early and then must devote many hours to practice and competition.

Obviously, some children find this time commitment excessive, and so they want to quit sport completely.

Is this because children are lazy? As children generally like to be active, this is doubtful. One reason might be that children are forced to specialize in activities that are inappropriate for them.

We have already discussed how growth spurts can affect a child's sporting life over a very short period of time.

Consider the case of Steve, who was identified as a "gifted" swimmer by his parents. To help him develop his swimming skills, he was put into an intensive training program. For two years he trained hard, averaging about twenty hours in the pool each week. At the age of fourteen, he suddenly grew six inches and started to develop more strength and power. With his new build and physical attributes, he was now a much better basketball or football prospect, yet his skills in those areas were poorly developed: he never had the time to develop them because of his swimming commitments. After two years of intensive swimming training, Steve was frustrated because the sports that he was now better suited for, and would probably find more enjoyable, were beyond his reach: he lacked the basic skills to compete effectively at a level appropriate for his age.

Is Steve an isolated case? Results from the Medford growth study, an impressive twelve-year investigation, suggest not. In that study, the sporting careers of young athletes were followed over a number of years. The results proved very interesting. Of all the athletes studied, only one out of four who were rated as sports "stars" in elementary school maintained that status three to four years later in junior high school. For various reasons, these early stars had been passed by children who didn't have this "star" status when they were younger.

There is a message here for B-parents. While the climb to the top in certain sports such as swimming and gymnastics requires an early specialization (it took Mary Lou Retton nine years to win an Olympic gold), parents should be wary of committing their child to any one intensive program too quickly. Early promise in one sport can often change quite rapidly because of physical changes in the child.

A much better approach is to introduce your children to as many different sporting activities as possible in their early years. Rather than trying to master the finer points of one sport, they should be encouraged to enjoy and become competent at a number of sports.

For those B-parents who think that this more general approach might be wasting precious learning time, note the following fact. Research has shown that children under ten years of age might benefit more in later years from motor skill training of a general, non-sport specific type (e.g., learning balance skills, inter-limb coordination skills, general strength development) than from sport-specific training (Rarick & Dobbins, 1975). You should keep this in mind when your children's sport careers are unfolding.

Pressures to Stay

The decision to leave sport, like a decision to leave anything that we have been involved with for some time, can be very difficult. For instance, one study examining the competitive experience of a number of young gymnasts revealed that a number of them found it extremely difficult to leave in spite of the fact that they were very unhappy while they were participating (Klint & Weiss, 1986).

Why were they afraid to quit? Some of their reasons included, "afraid of having extra time," "afraid of losing contact with sporting friends," and "afraid of being losers." While these may not seem like very "earth-shattering" reasons, it would be wrong for parents to minimize their importance. Parents should listen for signs that their children may want out of sport. Even if your children do not come right out and say that they want to quit, they may still be looking for a way out.

Look for these more indirect signs—complaints about the intensity of training, complaints about the time commitment, excessive emotional outbursts, unusual changes in mood, or injuries that don't seem to go away, even after appropriate treatment. In other words, look for signs that your children are not enjoying themselves any more.

If signs such as these start to appear, it would be wise if you sat down with your child and discussed the issue of leaving sport. By reassuring your child that sports leavers are not losers and that there is life after sport, you will be providing your child with an opportunity to leave sport graciously. You certainly would not want to be the parents of the gymnasts who confided that they may have deliberately injured themselves to provide the excuse they needed to leave gymnastics!

As this book is as much about enjoyment and feeling good about oneself as it is about sport, this seems like a fitting end. Being a good sporting parent means looking out for your children's interests as they enter, participate, and exit from sport. Hopefully, the information outlined in this book will allow you to "give your kids a sporting chance." If you remember the tenets of the A-parent, you will be well on your way to accomplishing this goal.

References and Other Readings

Ansorge, C.J., Sheer, J.K., Laub, J., & Howard, H.J. (1978).Bias in judging women's gymnastics induced by expectation of within-team order. *Research Quarterly*, 49, 399-405.

Bloom, B. (1982). The master teachers. *Phi Delta Kappan*, 63, 664-668.

Bloom, B. (1982). The role of gifts and markers in the development of talent. *Exceptional Children*, 48, 511-518.

Burton, D. (1983). *Evaluation of goal setting training on related cognitions and performance of collegiate swimmers.* Doctoral dissertaion, University of Illinois.

Burton, D., & Martens, R. (1986). Pinned by their own goals: An exploratory investigation into why kids drop out of wrestling. *Journal of Sport Psychology*, 8, 183-197.

Casady, M. (1974, Sept.). The tricky business of giving rewards. *Psychology Today*, p.52.

Chelladurai, P., & Carron, A.V. (1983). Athletic maturity and preferred leadership. *Journal of Sport Psychology*, 3, 85-92.

Clark, H.H. (1968). Characteristics of young athletes. *Kinesiology Review*, 33-42.

Coleman, J.S. (1961) *The adolescent society.* New York: The Free Press.

Deci, E.L. (1975). *Intrinsic motivation.* New York: Plenum.

Dryden, K. (1983). *The game.* Toronto: Macmillan.

Eitzen, D.S. (1975). Athletics in the status system of male adolescents: A replication of Coleman's 'The Adolescent Society.' *Alolescence*, 10, 267-276.

Ewing, M.W. (1981). *Achievement orientation and sport behavior of males and females.* Doctoral dissertation, University of Illinois.

Gill, D.L., Gross, J.B., & Huddleston, S. (1983). Participation motivation in youth sports. *International Journal of Sport Psychology*, 14, 1-14.

Gould, D., Feltz, D., Weiss, M. (1985). Motives for participating in competitive youth swimming. *International Journal of Sport Psychology*, 16, 126-140.

Gretzky, W., & Taylor, J. (1984). *Gretzky: From the back yard rink to the Stanley Cup.* Toronto: McClelland and Stewart.

Halliwell, W. (1978). Intrinsic motivation in sport. In W. F. Straub (Ed.), *Sport psychology: An analysis of athlete behavior.* Ithaca, NY: Mouvement.

Hull, B. (1967). *Hockey is my game.* Toronto: Longmans Canada Limited.

Klint, K.A., & Weiss, M.R. (1986). Dropping in and dropping out: Participation motives of current and former youth gymnasts. *Canadian Journal of Applied Sport Sciences*, 11, 106-114.

Longhurst, K., & Spink, J.S. (1987). Participation motivation of Australian children involved in organized sport. *Canadian Journal of Sport Sciences*, 12, 24-30.

Martens, R. (1980). *Parent guide to kids wrestling.* Champaign, IL: Human Kinetics.

Martens, R. (1978). *Joy and sadness in children's sports.* Champaign, IL: Human Kinetics.

Martens, R. (1977). *Sport competition anxiety test.* Champaign, IL: *Human Kinetics.*

Martens, R., & Seefeldt, V. (1979). *Guidelines for children's sports.* Washington, DC: AAHPERD Publications.

McClements, J.D., Fry, P.A.P., & Sefton, J. (1982). Research as a change agent in youth sport. In L. Wankel & R. B. Wilberg (Eds.), *Psychology of Sport and Motor Behavior: Research and Practice.* Proceedings of the Canadian Society for Psychomotor Learning and Sport Psychology: Fourteenth Annual Meetins. Edmonton, Alberta: University of Alberta.

McElroy, M.A. & Kirkendall, D.R. (1981). Conflict in perceived parent/child sport ablility judgments. *Journal of Sport Psychology*, 3, 244-247.

Mehrabian, A., & Bekken, M.L. (1986). Temperament characteristics of individuals who participate in strenuous sports. *Research Quarterly for Exercise and Sport*, 57, 160-166.

Miller, S.A. (1986) Parents' beliefs about their children's cognitive abilties. *Developmental Psychology*, 22, 276-284.

Miller Brewing Company (1983). *The Miller Lite report on American attitudes toward sports.* Milwaukee, WI: Author.

O'Reilly, D. (1975). *Mr. Hockey: The world of Gordie Howe.* Chicage: Henry Regnery Company.

Orlick, T., & Botterill, C. (1975). *Every kid can win.* Chicago: Nelson-Hall Publishers.

Orlick, T.D., & Mosher, R. (1978). Extrinsic rewards and participant motivation in a sport-related task. *International Journal of Sport Psychology*, 9, 27-39.

Orlick, T.D. & Parington, J., (1986). *Psych: Inner views of winning.* Ottawa: Coaching Association of Canada.

Passer, M.W., (1986). When should children begin competing? A Psychological perspective. In M.R. Weiss & D. Gould (Eds.), *Sport for children and youths.* Champaign, IL: Human Kinetics.

Peters, T.J., & Waterman, R.H. (1982). *In search of excellence: Lessons from America's best-run companies.* New York: Harper & Row.

Purdon, J. (1978). *Athletic participation and self-esteem.* Master's thesis, University of Western Ontario.

Rarick, G.L., & Dobbins, A.A. (1975). A motor performance typology of boys and girls in the age range 6 to 10 years. *Journal of Motor Behavior, 75,* 37-43.

Rejeski, W.J., Darracott, C., & Hutslar, S. (1979). Pygmalion in youth sports: A field study. *Journal of Sport Psychology,* 1, 311-319.

Retton, M.L. (1986). *Mary Lou: Creating an olympic champion.* New York: McGraw-Hill.

Rosenthal, R. & Jacobson, L. (1968). *Pygmalion in the classroom: Teacher expectation and pupils' intellectual development.* New York: Holt, Rinehart & Winston.

Scanlan, T.K., & Lewthwaite, R. (1984). Social psychological aspects of competition for male youth sport participants: 1. Predictors of competitive stress. *Journal of Sport Psychology,* 6, 208-226.

Scarisbrick, A.M., & Allison, M.T. (1986). The influence of competitive and recreational sport structures on children's perceived competence and enjoyment: The case of youth soccer. In J. Watkins, T. Reilly, & L. Burwitz (Eds.) *Sports Science: Proceedings of the VIII Commonwealth and International Conference on Sport, Physical Education, Dance, Recreation and Health.* London: E. & F.N. Spon.

Simon, J.A., & Martens, R. (1979). Children's anxiety in sport and nonsport evaluative activities. *Journal of Sport Psychology,* 1, 160-169.

Spink, K.S. (1986) *Coaching for sporting excellence: Enhancing the natural potential of children in sport.* Melbourne: Sun Books.

Spink, K.S. (1986) The effects of competitive orientation on the ability and effort attribution of racquetball players. *Behaviour Change,* 3, 94-99.

Thomas, J.R. (Ed.) (1977). *Youth sports guide for coaches and parents.* Washington, DC: AAHPERD Publications.

Weiss, M.R., & Gould, D., (Eds.) (1986). *Sport for children and youths.* Champaign, IL: Human Kinetics.